1 Impatient Perl

version: 22 February 2013

Copyright 2004-2013 Greg London

ISBN 978-1-300-77071-8

Permission is granted to copy, distribute and/or modify this document
under the terms of the GNU Free Documentation License, Version 1.3
or any later version published by the Free Software Foundation;
with no Invariant Sections, no Front-Cover Texts, and no Back-Cover Texts.
A copy of the license is included in the section entitled "GNU
Free Documentation License".

Cover Art (Front and Back) on the paperback version of Impatient Perl is excluded from this license.
Cover Art is Copyright Greg London 2004, All Rights Reserved.

For latest version of this work go to:
http://www.greglondon.com

Table of Contents

1 Impatient Perl..1
2 The Impatient Introduction to Perl...7
   2.1 The history of perl in 100 words or less..7
   2.2 Basic Formatting for this Document..8
   2.3 Do You Have Perl Installed..9
   2.4 Your First Perl Script, EVER..10
   2.5 Default Script Header..11
   2.6 Free Reference Material..11
   2.7 Cheap Reference Material...11
   2.8 Acronyms and Terms..12
3 Scalars...13
   3.1 Scalar Strings..14
      3.1.1 String Literals..14
      3.1.2 Single quotes versus Double quotes..14
      3.1.3 chomp..14
      3.1.4 concatenation...15
      3.1.5 repetition..15
      3.1.6 length...15
      3.1.7 substr (STRING_EXPRESSION, OFFSET, LENGTH);...........................15
      3.1.8 split..15
      3.1.9 join..16
      3.1.10 qw..16
      3.1.11 Multi-Line Strings, HERE Documents...17
   3.2 Scalar Numbers...18
      3.2.1 Numeric Literals..18
      3.2.2 Numeric Functions..18
      3.2.3 abs..18
      3.2.4 int...19
      3.2.5 trigonometry (sin,cos)...19
      3.2.6 exponentiation...20
      3.2.7 sqrt...20
      3.2.8 natural logarithms(exp,log)...20
      3.2.9 random numbers (rand, srand)..21
   3.3 Converting Between Strings and Numbers...21
      3.3.1 Stringify...22
      3.3.2 sprintf..22
      3.3.3 Numify...23
      3.3.4 oct..23
      3.3.5 hex..23
      3.3.6 Base Conversion Overview...24
   3.4 Undefined and Uninitialized Scalars..25
   3.5 Booleans..26
      3.5.1 FALSE...26
      3.5.2 TRUE..26
   3.6 Comparators...28
   3.7 Logical Operators...29

- 3.8 Default Values..29
- 3.9 Flow Control..30
- 3.10 Precedence...30
  - 3.10.1 Assignment Precedence...30
  - 3.10.2 Flow Control Precedence..31
- 3.11 Conditional Operator..31
- 3.12 References..33
- 3.13 Filehandles...34
- 3.14 Scalar Review..34

4 Arrays
- 4.1 scalar (@array)..36
- 4.2 push(@array, LIST)..37
- 4.3 pop(@array)...37
- 4.4 shift(@array)..38
- 4.5 unshift(@array, LIST)..38
- 4.6 foreach (@array)..39
- 4.7 sort(@array)..40
- 4.8 reverse(@array)...42
- 4.9 splice(@array)...42
- 4.10 Undefined and Uninitialized Arrays..42

5 Hashes
- 5.1 exists ($hash{$key})..44
- 5.2 delete ($hash{key})..45
- 5.3 keys(%hash)..46
- 5.4 values(%hash)...46
- 5.5 each(%hash)..47

6 List Context 51

7 References
- 7.1 Named Referents...54
- 7.2 References to Named Referents..54
- 7.3 Dereferencing..54
- 7.4 Anonymous Referents...56
- 7.5 Complex Data Structures..57
  - 7.5.1 Autovivification..58
  - 7.5.2 Multidimensional Arrays..59
  - 7.5.3 Deep Cloning, Deep Copy...60
- 7.6 Data Persistence...60
- 7.7 Stringification of References..60
- 7.8 The ref() function..62

8 Control Flow
- 8.1 Labels..65
- 8.2 last LABEL;...65
- 8.3 next LABEL;..65
- 8.4 redo LABEL;..65

9 Packages and Namespaces and Lexical Scoping
- 9.1 Package Declaration..66
- 9.2 Declaring Package Variables With our..67
- 9.3 Package Variables inside a Lexical Scope...68

- 9.4 Lexical Scope..........68
- 9.5 Lexical Variables..........69
- 9.6 Garbage Collection..........71
  - 9.6.1 Reference Count Garbage Collection..........72
  - 9.6.2 Garbage Collection and Subroutines..........72
- 9.7 Package Variables Revisited..........73
- 9.8 Calling local() on Package Variables..........74
- 10 Subroutines..........75
  - 10.1 Subroutine Sigil..........75
  - 10.2 Anonymous Subroutines..........77
  - 10.3 Data::Dumper and subroutines..........77
  - 10.4 Passing Arguments to/from a Subroutine..........77
  - 10.5 Accessing Arguments inside Subroutines via @_..........78
  - 10.6 Dereferencing Code References..........79
  - 10.7 Implied Arguments..........79
  - 10.8 Subroutine Return Value..........80
  - 10.9 Returning False..........81
  - 10.10 Using the caller() Function in Subroutines..........82
  - 10.11 The wantarray() function..........83
  - 10.12 Context Sensitive Subroutines with wantarray()..........83
- 11 Compiling and Interpreting..........84
- 12 Code Reuse, Perl Modules..........86
- 13 The use Statement..........87
- 14 The use Statement, Formally..........87
  - 14.1 The @INC Array..........88
  - 14.2 The use lib Statement..........88
  - 14.3 The PERL5LIB and PERLLIB Environment Variables..........88
  - 14.4 The require Statement..........89
  - 14.5 MODULENAME -> import (LISTOFARGS)..........89
  - 14.6 The use Execution Timeline..........90
- 15 bless()..........91
- 16 Method Calls..........93
  - 16.1 Inheritance..........95
  - 16.2 use base..........96
  - 16.3 INVOCANT->isa(BASEPACKAGE)..........97
  - 16.4 INVOCANT->can(METHODNAME)..........97
  - 16.5 Interesting Invocants..........98
- 17 Procedural Perl..........99
- 18 Object Oriented Perl..........99
  - 18.1 Class..........102
  - 18.2 SUPER..........103
  - 18.3 Object Destruction..........105
- 19 Object Oriented Review..........106
  - 19.1 Modules..........106
  - 19.2 use Module..........106
  - 19.3 bless / constructors..........107
  - 19.4 Methods..........108
  - 19.5 Inheritance..........108

- 19.6 Overriding Methods and SUPER...........108
- 19.7 Object Oriented and Moose.pm and Perl 6...........109
- 20 CPAN...........110
  - 20.1 CPAN, The Web Site...........110
  - 20.2 cpanm, The Perl Module Installer...........111
  - 20.3 Creating Modules for CPAN with Module::Starter...........111
- 21 The Next Level...........112
- 22 Command Line Arguments...........112
  - 22.1 @ARGV...........113
  - 22.2 Getopt::Declare...........115
    - 22.2.1 Getopt::Declare Sophisticated Example...........116
- 23 File Input and Output...........118
  - 23.1 close...........118
  - 23.2 read...........119
  - 23.3 write...........120
  - 23.4 File Tests...........120
  - 23.5 File Globbing...........120
  - 23.6 File Tree Searching...........121
- 24 Operating System Commands...........122
  - 24.1 The system() function...........122
  - 24.2 The Backtick Operator...........122
  - 24.3 Operating System Commands in a GUI...........123
- 25 Regular Expressions...........124
  - 25.1 Variable Interpolation...........125
  - 25.2 Wildcard Example...........126
  - 25.3 Defining a Pattern...........126
  - 25.4 Metacharacters...........127
  - 25.5 Capturing and Clustering Parenthesis...........129
    - 25.5.1 $1, $2, $3, etc Capturing parentheses...........129
    - 25.5.2 Capturing parentheses not capturing...........130
  - 25.6 Character Classes...........130
    - 25.6.1 Metacharacters Within Character Classes...........131
  - 25.7 Shortcut Character Classes...........131
  - 25.8 Greedy (Maximal) Quantifiers...........132
  - 25.9 Thrifty (Minimal) Quantifiers...........132
  - 25.10 Position Assertions / Position Anchors...........133
    - 25.10.1 The \b Anchor...........134
    - 25.10.2 The \G Anchor...........134
  - 25.11 Modifiers...........136
    - 25.11.1 Global Modifiers...........136
    - 25.11.2 The m And s Modifiers...........137
    - 25.11.3 The x Modifier...........138
  - 25.12 Modifiers For m{} Operator...........139
  - 25.13 Modifiers for s{}{} Operator...........139
  - 25.14 Modifiers for tr{}{} Operator...........139
  - 25.15 The qr{} function...........139
  - 25.16 Common Patterns...........139
  - 25.17 Regexp::Common...........140

25.18 Regexp::Grammars..140
26 Perl, GUI, and Tk...141
27 GNU Free Documentation License...142

2 The Impatient Introduction to Perl

This document is for people who either want to learn perl or are already programming in perl and just do not have the patience to scrounge for information to learn and use perl. This document should also find use as a handy desk reference for some of the more common perl related questions.

2.1 The history of perl in 100 words or less

In the mid 1980s, Larry Wall was working as a sys-admin and found that he needed to do a number of common, yet oddball functions over and over again. And he did not like any of the scripting languages that were around at the time, so he invented Perl. Version 1 was released circa 1987. A few changes have occurred between then and now. The current version of Perl has exceeded 5.8.3 and is a highly recommended upgrade.

Perl 6 is on the drawing board as a fundamental rewrite of the language. It was put on the drawing board in the year 2000. A decade later, it is still under development.

2.2 Basic Formatting for this Document

This document is formatted into text sections, code sections, and shell sections. This sentence is part of a text section. Text sections will extend to the far left margin and will use a non-monospaced font. Text sections contain descriptive text.

```
Code sections are indented.
They also use a monospaced font.
This is a code section, which represents
code to type into a script.
You will need to use a TEXT EDITOR,
not a WORD PROCESSOR to create these files.
Generally, the code is contained in one file,
and is executed via a shell command.

If the code section covers multiple files,
each file will be labeled.

###filename:MyFile.pm
This code will be placed in a
file called MyFile.pm

#!/usr/local/env perl
###filename:myscript.pl
This code will be placed in a file
called myscript.pl
The first line of myscript.pl will be the
line with #!/usr/local/env perl
```

```
> shell sections are indented like code sections
> shell sections also use monospaced fonts.
> shell sections differ from code sections in
> that shell sections start with a '>' character
> which represents a shell prompt.
> shell sections show commands to type on
> the command line.
> shell sections also show the output of a script,
> if any exists.
> In simple examples, the code is shown in a
> code section, immediately followed by the output
> from running the script. The command to run
> the script is dropped to save space.
```

As an example, the code for a simple "Hello World" script is shown here. It can be typed into a file of any name. The name of the file is not important. The command to execute the script is not important either. In this example, the code is important, and the output is important, so they are they only things shown.

```
print "Hello World\n";
> Hello World
```

THIS DOCUMENT REFERS TO (LI/U)NIX PERL ONLY. Much of this will translate to Mac Perl and Windows Perl, but the exact translation will be left as an exercise to the reader.

2.3 Do You Have Perl Installed

To find out if you have perl installed and its version:

```
> perl -v
```

You should have at least version 5.8.3. If you have an older version or if you have no perl installed at all, you can download it for free from

http://www.cpan.org

CPAN is an acronym for Comprehensive Perl Archive Network. The CPAN site contains the latest perl for download and installation, as well as a TON of perl modules for your use.

If you are a beginner, get your sys-admin to install perl for you. Even if you are not a beginner, get your sys-admin to install perl for you.

2.4 Your First Perl Script, EVER

Create a file called hello.pl using your favorite text editor. The .pl extension is simply a standard accepted extension for perl scripts. Type in the following:

```
#!/usr/bin/env perl
use warnings;
use strict; # comment
print "Hello World \n";
```

Run the script:

```
> perl hello.pl
Hello World
```

This calls perl and passes it the name of the script to execute.

The #! on the first line is sometimes pronounced "shebang". Anything from a # character to the end of the line is a comment. So, the shebang on the first line is a comment. But the shebang also happens to be a secret handshake interpreter directive to tell the program loader in Unix-type systems to pass the rest of the script to whatever is after the #! part, in our case, /usr/bin/env perl.

If you call the script with perl hello.pl then you don't need the shebang line at the beginning of the script. But, if you have the shebang line on the first line of your script, and you're on a Unix-like system, you can run the script directly on the command line.

First, make the file executable:

```
> chmod +x hello.pl
```

Then run the script directly.

```
> hello.pl
Hello World
```

If "." is not in your PATH variable, you will have to run the script by typing:

```
> ./hello.pl
```

HOORAY! Now go update your resume.

2.5 Default Script Header

All the code examples in this document are assumed to have the following script header, unless otherwise stated. It uses your PATH environment variable to determine which perl executable to run. If you need to have different versions of perl installed on your system, you can control which version of perl they will run by changing your PATH variable without having to change your script.

```
#!/usr/bin/env perl
use warnings;
use strict;
use Data::Dumper;
```

Note that Data::Dumper takes some time to load and you wouldn't want to use Data::Dumper on some timing-critical project. But for learning perl with simple scripts, the execution speed isn't that high of a priority. If you're writing a 途ealscript (i.e. one where time-to-run and memory-usage are issues to be considered), then don't use Data::Dumper by default, only use it if you really need it.

2.6 Free Reference Material

You can get quick help from the standard perl installation.

```
> perl -h
> perldoc
> perldoc -h
> perldoc perldoc
```

FAQs on CPAN: http://www.cpan.org/cpan-faq.html
Mailing Lists on CPAN: http://list.cpan.org
More free documentation on the web: http://www.perldoc.com
Still more free documentation on the web: http://learn.perl.org

2.7 Cheap Reference Material

"Programming Perl" by Larry Wall, Tom Christiansen, and Jon Orwant. Highly recommended book to have handy at all times. It is sometimes referred to as the "Camel Book" by way of the camel drawing on its cover. The publisher, O'Reilly, has printed enough computer books to choke a, well, camel, and each one has a different animal on its cover. Therefore if you hear reference to some animal book, it is probably an O'Reilly book. Well, unless its the "Dragon Book", because that refers to a book called "Compilers" by Aho, Sethi, and Ullman.

2.8 Acronyms and Terms

Perl: Originally, "Pearl" shortened to "Perl" to gain status as a 4-letter word. Now considered an acronym for Practical Extraction and Report Language, as well as Petty Eclectic Rubbish Lister. The name was invented first. The acronyms followed. Note that this is "Perl" with a capital "P". The "perl" with a lower case "p" refers to the executable found somewhere near /usr/local/bin/perl

CPAN: Comprehensive Perl Archive Network. (http://www.cpan.org) Before you write anything in perl, check cpan to see if someone already wrote it for you.

DWIM: Do What I Mean. Once upon a time, the standard mantra for computer inflexibility was this: "I really hate this darn machine, I wish that they would sell it. It never does what I want, but only what I tell it." DWIM-iness is an attempt to embed perl with telepathic powers such that it can understand what you wanted to write in your code even though you forgot to actually type it. Well, alright, DWIM is just a way of saying the language was designed by some really lazy programmers so that you could be even lazier than they were. (They had to write perl in C, so they could not be TOO lazy.)

AUTOVIVIFY: "auto" meaning "self". "vivify" meaning "alive". To bring oneself to life. Generally applies to perl variables that can grant themselves into being without an explicit declaration from the programmer. Part of perl's DWIM-ness. "Autovivify" is a verb. The noun form is "autovivification". Sometimes, autovivification is not what you meant your code to do, and for some reason, when "do what I mean" meets autovivification in perl, autovivification wins.

And now, a Haiku:
```
Do What I Mean and
Autovivification
sometimes unwanted
```

TMTOWTDI: There is More Than One Way To Do It. An acknowledgment that any programming problem has more than one solution. Rather than have perl decide which solution is best, it gives you all the tools and lets you choose. This allows a programmer to select the tool that will let him get his job done. Sometimes, it gives a perl newbie just enough rope to hang himself.

Foo Fighters: A phrase used around the time of WWII by radar operators to describe a signal that could not be explained. Later became known as a UFO. This has nothing to do with perl, except that "foo" is a common variable name used in perl.

Fubar: Another WWII phrase used to indicate that a mission had gone seriously awry or that a piece of equipment was inoperative. An acronym for Fouled Up Beyond All Recognition and similar interpretations. This has nothing to do with perl either, except that fubar somehow got mangled into foobar, and perl is often awash in variables named "foo" and "bar", especially if the programmer wishes to hide the fact that he did not understand his code well enough to come up with better names.

If you use a $foo variable in your code, you deserve to maintain it.

Storage

Perl has three basic storage types: Scalars, Arrays, and Hashes.
The most basic storage type is a Scalar.
Arrays and Hashes use Scalars to build more complex data types.

3 Scalars

Scalars are preceded with a dollar sign sigil. A "$" is a stylized "S".

sigil : A symbol. In Perl, sigil refers to the symbol in front of a variable.

Scalars can store Strings, Numbers (integers and floats), References, and Filehandles. Perl is smart enough to know which type you are putting into a scalar and handle it.

```
my $diameter = 42;       # The 'my' keyword declares a lexical
my $pi = 3.1415;         # variable. If you don't know what
my $initial = 'g';       # that means, don't worry about it,
my $name = 'John Doe';   # it will be explained later.
my $ref_to_name = \$name # Specifically, in section 4
```

Without "use strict;" and without declaring a variable with a "my", using the name of a new variable causes perl to create that variable silently and initialize it to undef. This undef value will stringify to "" or numify to 0, depending how the undefined variable is used. This is called autovivication. (Stringification and Numification are covered later.)

Autovivify : to bring oneself to life.

In some situations, autovivication is handy. However, in certain situations, autovivification can be an unholy monster.

```
my $pi = 3.1415;
my $diameter = 42;
my $circumference = $pie * $diameter;
# oops, $pie doesn't exist. Autovivified to undef,
# numified to 0, therefore $circumference is zero.
```

Without use warnings; use strict; perl will autovivify a new variable called "pie", initialize it to zero, and assume that is what you meant to do. There is no reason that warnings and strictness should not be turned on in your scripts.

3.1 Scalar Strings

Scalars can store strings. You do not have to declare the length of the string, perl just handles it for you automatically.

3.1.1 String Literals

String literals must be in single or double quotes or you will get an error.

```
print hello;
Error: Unquoted string "hello" may clash with
reserved word
```

You can use single quotes or double quotes to set off a string literal:

```
my $name = 'mud';
my $greeting = "hello, $name\n";
print $greeting;
> hello, mud
```

You can also create a list of string literals using the qw() function.

```
my ($first,$last)=qw( John Doe );
print "first is '$first'\n";
print "last is '$last'\n";
> first is 'John'
> last is 'Doe'
```

3.1.2 Single quotes versus Double quotes

Single quoted strings are a "what you see is what you get" kind of thing.

```
my $name = 'mud';
print 'hello $name';
> hello $name
```

Double quotes means that you get SOME variable interpolation during string evaluation. Complex variables, such as a hash lookup, will not be interpolated properly in double quotes.

```
my $name = 'mud';
print "hello $name \n";
> hello mud
```

Note: a double-quoted "\n" is a new-line character.

3.1.3 chomp

You may get rid of a newline character at the end of a string by chomp-ing the string. The chomp function removes one new line from the end of the string even if there are multiple newlines at the end. If there are no newlines, chomp leaves the string alone. The return value of chomp is what was chomped (seldom used).

```
My $string = "hello world\n";
chomp($string);
warn "string is '$string' \n"
> string is 'hello world' ...
```

3.1.4 concatenation

String concatenation uses the period character ".".

```
my $fullname = 'mud' . "bath";
```

3.1.5 repetition

Repeat a string with the "x" operator.

```
my $line = '-' x 80; # $line is eighty hypens
```

3.1.6 length

Find out how many characters are in a string with length().

```
my $len = length($line); # $len is 80
```

3.1.7 substr (STRING_EXPRESSION, OFFSET, LENGTH);

Spin, fold, and mutilate strings using substr(). The substr function gives you fast access to get and modify chunks of a string. You can quickly get a chunk of LENGTH characters starting at OFFSET from the beginning or end of the string (negative offsets go from the end). The substr function then returns the chunk.

```
my $chunk = substr('the rain in spain', 9, 2);
warn "chunk is '$chunk'";
> chunk is 'in' ...
```

The substr function can also be assigned to, replacing the chunk as well. You need a string contained in a variable that can be modified, rather than using a constant literal in the example above.

```
my $string = 'the rain in spain';
substr($string, 9, 2) = 'beyond';
warn "string is '$string'";
> string is 'the rain beyond spain' ...
```

3.1.8 split

Use the split function to break a string expression into components when the components are separated by a common substring pattern.

```
split(/PATTERN/, STRING_EXPRESSION,LIMIT);
```

For example, tab separated data in a single string can be split into separate strings.

```
my $tab_sep_data = "John\tDoe\tmale\t42";
my ($first,$last,$gender,$age)= split(/\t/, $tab_sep_data);
```

You can break a string into individual characters by calling split with an empty string pattern "". The /PATTERN/ in split() is a Regular Expression, which is complicated enough to get its own chapter. However, some common regular expression PATTERNS for split are:

```
\t tab-separated data
\s+ whitespace-separated data
\s*,\s* comma-separated data
```

3.1.9 join

Use join to stitch a list of strings into a single string.

```
join('SEPARATOR STRING', STRING1, STRING2, ...);
```

For example:

```
my $string = join(" and ",
'apples', 'bananas', 'peaches');
warn "string is '$string'";
> string is 'apples and bananas and peaches'...
```

3.1.10 qw

The qw() function takes a list of barewords and quotes them for you.

```
my $string = join(" and ", qw(apples bananas peaches));
warn "string is '$string'";
> string is 'apples and bananas and peaches'...
```

3.1.11 Multi-Line Strings, HERE Documents

Perl allows you to place a multi-line string in your code by using what it calls a "here document

```
My $string = <<'ENDOFDOCUMENT';
Do What I Mean and
Autovivification
sometimes unwanted
ENDOFDOCUMENT

warn "string is '$string'
> string is 'Do What I Mean and
> Autovivification
> sometimes unwanted' at ...
```

The '<<' indicates a HERE document, followed by the name of the label indicating the end of the here document. Enclosing the label in double quotes means that perl variables in the document will get interpolated as strings. Enclosing the label in single quotes means that no string interpolation occurs.

Perl then reads the lines after the '<<' as string literal content until it sees the end of string label positioned at the beginning of a line.

3.2 Scalar Numbers

Perl generally uses floats internally to store numbers. If you specify something that is obviously an integer, it will use an integer. Either way, you simply use it as a scalar.

```
my $days_in_week = 7; # scalar => integer
my $temperature = 98.6; # scalar => float
```

3.2.1 Numeric Literals

Perl allows several different formats for numeric literals, including integer, floating point, and scientific notation, as well as decimal, octal, and hexadecimal.
Binary numbers begin with "0b"
hexadecimal numbers begin with "0x"
Octal number begin with a "0"
All other numeric literals are assumed to be decimal.

```
my $solar_temp_c = 1.5e7; # centigrade
my $solar_temp_f = 27_000_000.0; # Fahrenheit
my $base_address = 01234567; # octal
my $high_address = 0xfa94; # hexadecimal
my $low_address = 0b100101; # binary
```

3.2.2 Numeric Functions

3.2.3 abs

Use abs to get the absolute value of a number.

```
my $var1 = abs(-3.4); # var1 is 3.4
my $var2 = abs(5.9); # var2 is 5.9
```

3.2.4 int

Use "int" to convert a floating point number to an integer. Note that this truncates everything after the decimal point, which means you do NOT get rounding. Truncating means that positive numbers always get smaller and negative numbers always get bigger.

```
my $price = 9.95;
my $dollars = int ($price);
# dollars is 9, not 10! false advertising!
my $y_pos = -5.9;
my $y_int = int($y_pos);
# y_int is -5 (-5 is "bigger" than -5.9)
```

If you want to round a float to the nearest integer, you will need to write a bit of code. One way to accomplish it is to use sprintf:

```
my $price = 9.95;
my $dollars = sprintf("%.0f", $price);
# dollars is 10
```

3.2.5 trigonometry (sin,cos)

The sin() and cos() functions return the sine and cosine of a value given in RADIANS. If you have a value in DEGREES, multiply it by (pi/180) first.

```
my $angle = 45; # 45 deg
my $radians = $angle * ( 3.14 / 180 ); # .785 rad
my $sine_rad = sin($radians); # 0.707 Correct!
my $sine_deg = sin($angle); # 0.851 OOPS!
```

If you need inverse sine, inverse cosine, or tangent then use the Math::Trig module on CPAN.

3.2.6 exponentiation

Use the "**" operator to raise a number to some power.

```
my $seven_squared = 7 ** 2; # 49
my $five_cubed = 5 ** 3; #125
my $three_to_the_fourth = 3 ** 4; # 81
Use fractional powers to take a root of a number:
my $square_root_of_49 = 49 ** (1/2); # 7
my $cube_root_of_125 = 125 ** (1/3); # 5
my $fourth_root_of_81 = 81 ** (1/4); # 3
```

Standard perl cannot handle imaginary numbers. Use the Math::Complex module on CPAN.

3.2.7 sqrt

Use sqrt to take the square root of a positive number.

```
my $square_root_of_123 = sqrt(123); # 11.0905
```

3.2.8 natural logarithms(exp,log)

The exp function returns e to the power of the value given. To get e, call exp(1);

```
my $value_of_e = exp(1); # 2.7183
my $big_num= exp(42); # 2.7183 ** 42 = 1.7e18
```

The log function returns the inverse exp() function, which is to say, log returns the number to which you would have to raise e to get the value passed in.

```
my $inv_exp = log($big_num); # inv_exp = 42
```

3.2.9 random numbers (rand, srand)

The rand function is a pseudorandom number generator (PRNG).

If a value is passed in, rand returns a float that satisfies (0 <= return < input)

If no value is passed in, rand returns a float in the range (0 <= return < 1)

if you want a random integer in the range of (0..$max), then you'll need to convert it to int(), (and remember int() truncates which is what we want here) like this:

```
my $rnd = int(rand($max+1));
```

The srand function will seed the PRNG with the value passed in. If no value is passed in, srand will seed the PRNG with something from the system that will give it decent randomness. You can pass in a fixed value to guarantee the values returned by rand will always follow the same sequence (and therefore are predictable). You should only need to seed the PRNG once. If you have a version of perl greater than or equal to 5.004, you should not need to call it at all, because perl will call srand at startup.

3.3 Converting Between Strings and Numbers

Many languages require the programmer to explicitly convert numbers to strings before printing them out and to convert strings to numbers before performing arithmetic on them. Perl is not one of these languages.

Perl will attempt to apply Do What I Mean to your code and just Do The Right Thing. There are two basic conversions that can occur: stringification and numification.

3.3.1 Stringify

Stringify: Converting something other than a string to a string form.
Perl will automatically convert a number (integer or floating point) to a string format before printing it out.

```
my $mass = 7.3;
my $volume = 4;
warn "mass is '$mass'\n";
warn "volume is '$volume'\n";
> mass is '7.3' ...
> volume is '4' ...
```

Even though $mass is stored internally as a floating point number and $volume is stored internally as an integer, the code did not have to explicitly convert these numbers to string format before printing them out. Perl will attempt to convert the numbers into the appropriate string representation. If you do not want the default format, use sprintf. If you want to force stringification, simply concatenate a null string onto the end of the value.

```
my $mass = 7.3; # 7.3
my $string_mass = $mass .= ''; # '7.3'
```

3.3.2 sprintf

Use sprintf to control exactly how perl will convert a number into string format.

```
sprintf ( FORMAT_STRING, LIST_OF_VALUES );
```

For example:

```
my $pi = 3.1415;
my $str = sprintf("%06.2f",$pi);
warn "str is '$str'";
> str is '003.14' ...
```

Decoding the above format string:

```
%  => format
0  => fill leading spaces with zero
6  => total length, including decimal point
.2 => put two places after the decimal point
f  => floating point notation
```

To convert a number to a hexadecimal, octal, binary, or decimal formated string, use the following FORMAT_STRINGS:

```
hexadecimal "%lx"   The letter 'l' (L)
octal "%lo"         indicates the input is
binary "%lb"        an integer, possibly
decimal integer "%ld"  a Long integer.
decimal float "%f"
scientific "%e"
```

3.3.3 Numify

Numify: Converting something other than a number to a numeric form.
Sometimes you have string information that actually represents a number. For example, a user might enter the string "19.95" which must be converted to a float before perl can perform any arithmetic on it.

You can force numification of a value by adding integer zero to it.

```
my $user_input = '19.95';       # '19.95'
my $price = $user_input+0;      # 19.95
```

If the string is NOT in base ten format, then use oct() or hex()

3.3.4 oct

The oct function can take a string that fits the octal, hexadecimal, or binary format and convert it to an integer.

binary formatted strings must start with "0b"

hexadecimal formatted strings must start with "0x"

All other numbers are assumed to be octal strings.

Note: even though the string might not start with a zero (as required by octal literals), oct will assume the string is octal. This means calling oct() on a decimal number could be a bad thing.

To handle a string that could contain octal, hexadecimal, binary, OR decimal strings, you could assume that octal strings must start with "0". Then, if the string starts with zero, call oct on it, else assume it's decimal. This example uses regular expressions and the conditional operator.

```
my $num = ($str=~m{^0}) ? oct($str) : $str + 0;
```

3.3.5 hex

The hex() function takes a string in hex format and converts it to integer. The hex() function is like oct() except that hex() only handles hex base strings, and it does not require a "0x" prefix.

3.3.6 Base Conversion Overview

Given a decimal number:

```
my $decimal=12;
```

Convert from decimal to another base using sprintf:

```
my $hex = sprintf("%lx", $decimal);
my $oct = sprintf("%lo", $decimal);
my $bin = sprintf("%lb", $decimal);
```

If you want to pad the most significant bits with zeroes and you know the width, use this:

```
# 08 assumes width is 8 characters
my $p_hex = sprintf("%08lx", $decimal);
my $p_oct = sprintf("%08lo", $decimal);
my $p_bin = sprintf("%08lb", $decimal);
```

If you have a string and you want to convert it to decimal, use the conditional operator and oct().

```
sub convert_to_decimal {
  ($_[0]=~m{^0}) ? Oct($_[0]) : $_[0] + 0;
}

warn convert_to_decimal('42'); # dec
warn convert_to_decimal('032'); # oct
warn convert_to_decimal('0xff'); # hex
warn convert_to_decimal('0b1001011'); # bin
```

If you want to know how many bits it would take to store a number, convert it to binary using sprintf (don't pad with zeros) and then call length() on it.

```
warn length(sprintf("%lb", 255)); # 8
```

3.4 Undefined and Uninitialized Scalars

All the examples above initialized the scalars to some known value before using them. You can declare a variable but not initialize it, in which case, the variable is undefined. If you use a scalar that is undefined, perl will stringify or numify it based on how you are using the variable.

An undefined scalar stringifies to an empty string: ""

An undefined scalar numifies to zero: 0

Without warnings or strict turned on, this conversion is silent. With warnings/strict on, the conversion still takes place, but a warning is emitted.

Since perl automatically performs this conversion no matter what, there is no string or numeric operation that will die if it tries to do math on an undefined variable. So, its up to you to check that your variables are defined if there is a chance they may be undefined.

Use the defined() function to test whether a scalar is defined or not.

If the scalar is defined, the function returns a boolean "true" (1)

If the scalar is NOT defined, the function returns a boolean "false" ("").

If you have a scalar with a defined value in it, and you want to return it to its uninitialized state, assign undef to it. This will be exactly as if you declared the variable with no initial value.

```
my $var; # undef
print "test 1 :";
if(defined($var)) {print "defined\n";}
   else {print "undefined\n";}
$var = 42; # defined
print "test 2 :";
if(defined($var)) {print "defined\n";}
   else {print "undefined\n";}
$var = undef; # undef as if never initialized
print "test 3 :";
if(defined($var)) {print "defined\n";}
   else {print "undefined\n";}
> test 1 :undefined
> test 2 :defined
> test 3 :undefined
```

3.5 Booleans

Perl does not have a boolean "type" per se. Instead, perl interprets scalar strings and numbers as "true" or "false" based on some rules:

```
1) Strings "" and "0" are FALSE,
   any other string or stringification is TRUE
2) Number 0 is FALSE, any other number is TRUE
3) all references are TRUE
4) undef is FALSE
```

Note that these are SCALARS. Any variable that is not a SCALAR is first evaluated in scalar context, and then treated as a string or number by the above rules. The scalar context of an ARRAY is its size. An array with a hundred undef values has a scalar() value of 100 and is therefore evaluated as TRUE.

A subroutine returns a scalar or a list depending on the context in which it is called. To explicitly return FALSE in a subroutine, use this:

```
return wantarray() ? () : 0; # FALSE
```

This is sufficiently troublesome to type for such a common thing that an empty return statement within a subroutine will do the same thing:

```
return; #FALSE
```

3.5.1 FALSE

The following scalars are interpreted as FALSE:

```
integer 0 # false
float 0.0 # false
string '0' # false
string '' # false
undef # false
```

3.5.2 TRUE

ALL other values are interpreted as TRUE, which means the following scalars are considered TRUE, even though you might not have expected them to be false.

```
string '0.0' # true
string '00' # true
string 'false' # true
float 3.1415 # true
integer 11 # true
string 'yowser' # true
```

If you are doing a lot of work with numbers on a variable, you may wish to force numification on that variable ($var+0) before it gets boolean tested, just in case you end up with a string "0.0" instead of a float 0.0 and get some seriously hard to find bugs.

Note that the string '0.0' is TRUE, but ('0.0'+0) will get numified to 0, which is FALSE. If you are processing a number as a string and want to evaluate it as a BOOLEAN, make sure you explicitly NUMIFY it before testing its BOOLEANNESS.

Built in Perl functions that return a boolean will return an integer one (1) for TRUE and an empty string ("") for FALSE.

3.6 Comparators

Comparison operators return booleans, specifically an integer 1 for true and a null string "" for false. The "Comparison" operator ("<=>" and "cmp") return a -1, 0, or +1, indicating the compared values are less than, equal to, or greater than. Distinct comparison operators exist for comparing strings and for comparing numbers.

```
String   Numeric   equal to
------   -------   --------------------------
eq       ==        equal to
ne       !=        not equal to
lt       <         less than
gt       >         greater than
le       <=        less than or equal to
ge       >=        greater than or equal to
cmp      <=>       comparison(lt=-1,eq=0,gt=1)
```

Note that if you use a string operator to compare two numbers, you will get their alphabetical string comparison. Perl will stringify the numbers and then perform the compare. This will occur silently; perl will emit no warning. And if you wanted the numbers compared numerically but used string comparison, then you will get the wrong result when you compare the strings ("9" lt "100").

String "9" is greater than (gt) string "100".

Number 9 is less than (<=) number 100.

If you use a numeric operator to compare two strings, perl will attempt to numify the strings and then compare them numerically. Comparing "John" <= "Jacob" will cause perl to convert "John" into a number and fail miserably. However, if warnings/strict is not on, it will fail miserably and SILENTLY, assigning the numification of "John" to integer zero.

The numeric comparison operator '<=>' is sometimes called the "spaceship operator". If you squint, it looks like a flying saucer.

3.7 Logical Operators

Perl has two sets of operators to perform logical AND, OR, NOT functions. The difference between the two is that one set has a higher precedence than the other set.

The higher precedence logical operators are the '&&', '||', and '!' operators.

```
Op function    return value
-- --------    ------------------------------------
&& (AND)       if ($one is false) $one else $two
|| (OR)        if ($one is true) $one else $two
!  (NOT)       if ($one is false) true else false
```

The lower precedence logical operators are the 'and', 'or', 'not', and 'xor' operators.

```
Op         function    return value
---        --------    -----------------------------
and        (AND)       if ($one is false) $one else $two
or         (OR)        if ($one is true) $one else $two
not        (NOT)       if ($one is false) true else false
xor        (XOR)       if ( ($one true and $two false) or
                           ($one false and $two true) ) then
                       return true else false
```

Both sets of operators are very common in perl code, so it is useful to learn how precedence affects their behavior. But first, some examples of how to use them.

3.8 Default Values

This subroutine has two input parameters ($left and $right) with default values (1.0 and 2.0). If the user calls the subroutine with missing arguments, the undefined parameters will instead receive their default values.

```
sub mysub {
   my( $left, $right )=@_;
   $left ||= 1.0;
   $right ||= 2.0;
   # deal with $left and $right here.
}
```

The '||=' operator is a fancy shorthand. This:
```
$left ||= 1.0;
```

is exactly the same as this:
```
$left = $left || 1.0;
```

3.9 Flow Control

The open() function here will attempt to open $filename for reading and attach $filehandle to it. If open() fails in any way, it returns FALSE, and FALSE OR'ed with die () means that perl will evaluate the die() function to finish the logical evaluation. It won't complete because execution will die, but the end result is code that is actually quite readable.

```
open (my $filehandle, $filename)
    or die "cant open";
```

3.10 Precedence

The reason we used '||' in the first example and 'or' in the second example is because the operators have different precedence, and we used the one with the precedence we needed.

3.10.1 Assignment Precedence

When working with an assignment, use '||' and '&&', because they have a higher precedence than (and are evaluated before) the assignment '='. The 'or' and 'and' operators have a precedence that is LOWER than an assignment, meaning the assignment would occur first, followed by any remaining 'and' and 'or' operators.

Right:

```
my $default = 0 || 1;
# default is 1
```

Wrong:

```
my $default = 0 or 1;
# default is 0
```

The second (wrong) example is equivalent to this:

```
(my $default = 0) or 1;
```

which will ALWAYS assign $default to the first value and discard the second value.

3.10.2 Flow Control Precedence

When using logical operators to perform flow control, use 'or' and 'and' operators, because they have lower precedence than functions and other statements that form the boolean inputs to the 'or' or 'and' operator. The '||' and '&&' have higher precedence than functions and may execute before the first function call.

Right:
```
close $fh or die "Error:could not close";
```

Wrong:
```
close $fh || die "Error: could not close";
```

The second (wrong) example is equivalent to this:
```
close ($fh || die "Error");
```

which will ALWAYS evaluate $fh as true, NEVER die, and close $fh. If close() fails, the return value is discarded, and the program continues on its merry way.

It is always possible to override precedence with parentheses, but it is probably better to get in the habit of using the right operator for the right job.

3.11 Conditional Operator

The conditional operator mimics the conditional testing of an if-else block. The conditional operator uses three operands, and is also called a trinary operator.

As it happens, the conditional operator is perl's ONLY trinary operator, so people sometimes call it the trinary or ternary operator when they mean conditional operator. As long as perl doesn't add another trinary operator, its not a problem. It is even more rarely called the ?: operator.

The conditional operator has this form:
```
my $RESULT = $BOOLEAN1 ? $VALUE1 : $VALUE2;
```

This can be rewritten as an if-else block like this:
```
my $RESULT;
if($BOOLEAN1) {
   $RESULT = $VALUE1
} else {
   $RESULT = $VALUE2
}
```

The conditional operator allows you to declare the variable and perform the assignment all in one short line of code.

Note that $BOOLEAN1, $VALUE1 and $VALUE2 can be replaced by any normal perl expression, rather than being limited to a simple scalar value. One interesting expression that you could replace $VALUE2 with is another conditional operator, effectively allowing you to create a chain of if-elsif-elsif-else statements. For example:

```
my $RESULT =
  $BOOLEAN1 ? $VALUE1
: $BOOLEAN2 ? $VALUE2
: $BOOLEAN3 ? $VALUE3
: $BOOLEAN4 ? $VALUE4
: $VALUE5;
```

The above example is equivalent to this mouthful:

```
my $RESULT;
   if($BOOLEAN1) { $RESULT = $VALUE1 }
elsif($BOOLEAN2) { $RESULT = $VALUE2 }
elsif($BOOLEAN3) { $RESULT = $VALUE3 }
elsif($BOOLEAN4) { $RESULT = $VALUE4 }
eles { $RESULT = $VALUE5 }
```

3.12 References

A reference points to the variable to which it refers. It is kind of like a pointer in C, which says "the data I want is at this address". Unlike C, you cannot manually alter the address of a perl reference. You can only create a reference to a variable that is visible from your current scope.

Create a reference by placing a "\" in front of the variable:

```
my $name = 'John';
my $age = 42;
my $name_ref = \$name;
my $age_ref = \$age;
```

Perl will stringify a reference so that you can print it and see what it is.

```
warn "age_ref is '$age_ref'";
> age_ref is 'SCALAR(0x812e6ec)' ...
```

This tells you that $age_ref is a reference to a SCALAR (which we know is called $age). It also tells you the address of the variable to which we are referring is 0x812e6ec.

You cannot referencify a string. I.E. you cannot give perl a string, such as "SCALAR (0x83938949)" and have perl give you a reference to whatever is at that address. Perl is pretty loosy goosey about what it will let you do, but not even perl is so crazy as to give people complete access to the system memory.

You can dereference a reference by putting an extra sigil (of the appropriate type) in front of the reference variable.

```
my $name = 'John';
my $ref_to_name = \$name;
my $deref_name = $$ref_to_name;
warn $deref_name;
> John ...
```

References are interesting enough that they get their own section. But I introduce them here so that I can introduce a really cool module that uses references: Data::Dumper. Data::Dumper will take a reference to ANYTHING and print out the thing to which it refers in a human readable form.

This does not seem very impressive with a reference to a scalar:

```
my $name = 'John';
my $ref_to_name = \$name;
warn Dumper \$ref_to_name;
> $VAR1 = \'John';
```

But this will be absolutely essential when working with Arrays and Hashes.

3.13 Filehandles

Scalars can store a filehandle. File IO gets its own section, but I introduce it here to give a complete picture of what scalars can hold.

Given a scalar that is undefined (uninitialized), calling open() on that scalar and a string filename will tell perl to open the file specified by the string, and store the handle to that file in the scalar.

```
open(my $fh, '>out.txt');
print $fh "hello world\n";
print $fh "this is simple file writing\n";
close($fh);
```

The scalar $fh in the example above holds the filehandle to "out.txt". Printing to the filehandle actually outputs the string to the file.

There is some magic going on there that I have not explained, but that is a quick intro to scalar filehandles.

3.14 Scalar Review

Scalars can store STRINGS, NUMBERS (floats and ints), REFERENCES, and FILEHANDLES.

Stringify: to convert something to a string format

Numify: to convert something to a numeric format

The following scalars are interpreted as boolean FALSE:

integer 0, float 0.0, string "0", string "", undef

All other scalar values are interpreted as boolean TRUE.

4 Arrays

Arrays are preceded with an "at" sigil. The "@" is a stylized "a".

An array stores a bunch of scalars that are accessed via an integer index.

Perl arrays are ONE-DIMENSIONAL ONLY. (Do Not Panic.)

The first element of an array always starts at ZERO (0).

When you refer to an entire array, use the "@" sigil.

```
my @numbers = qw ( zero one two three );
```

When you index into the array, the "@" character changes to a "$" and the numeric index is placed in square brackets.

```
my @numbers = qw ( zero one two three );
my $string = $numbers[2];
warn $string;
> two ...
```

The length of an array is not pre-declared. Perl autovivifies whatever space it needs.

```
my @months;
$months[1]='January';
$months[5]='May';
# $months[0] and $months[2..4] are autovivified
# and initialized to undef
print Dumper \@months;
> $VAR1 = [
>   undef,              # index 0 is undefined
>   'January',          # $months[1]
>   ${\$VAR1->[0]},     # this is same as undef
>   ${\$VAR1->[0]},     # undef
>   ${\$VAR1->[0]},     # undef
>   'May'               # $months[5]
>   ];
```

If you want to see if you can blow your memory, try running this piece of code:

```
my @mem_hog;
$mem_hog[1000000000000000000000]=1;

# the array is filled with undefs
# except the last entry, which is initialized to 1
```

Arrays can store ANYTHING that can be stored in a scalar

```
my @junk_drawer = ( 'pliers', 1,1,1, '*', '//',
    3.14, 9*11, 'yaba', 'daba' );
```

Negative indexes start from the end of the array and work backwards.

```
my @colors = qw ( red green blue );
my $last=$colors[-1];
warn "last is '$last'";
> last is 'blue' ...
```

4.1 scalar (@array)

To get how many elements are in the array, use "scalar"

```
my @phonetic = qw ( alpha bravo charlie delta );
my $quantity = scalar(@phonetic);
warn $quantity;
> 4 ...
```

When you assign an entire array into a scalar variable, you will get the same thing, but calling scalar() is much more clear.

```
my @phonetic = qw ( alpha bravo charlie );
my $quant = @phonetic;
warn $quant;
> 3 ...
```

This is explained later in the "list context" section.

4.2 push(@array, LIST)

Use push() to add elements onto the end of the array (the highest index). This will increase the length of the array by the number of items added.

```
my @groceries = qw ( milk bread );
push(@groceries, qw ( eggs bacon cheese ));
print Dumper \@groceries;
```

```
> $VAR1 = [
> 'milk',
> 'bread',
> 'eggs',
> 'bacon',
> 'cheese'
> ];
```

4.3 pop(@array)

Use pop() to get the last element off of the end of the array (the highest index). This will shorten the array by one. The return value of pop() is the value popped off of the array.

```
my @names = qw ( alice bob charlie );
my $last_name = pop(@names);
warn "popped = $last_name";
print Dumper \@names;
> popped = charlie ...
> $VAR1 = [
> 'alice',
> 'bob'
> ];
```

4.4 shift(@array)

Use shift() to remove one element from the beginning/bottom of an array (i.e. at index zero). All elements will be shifted DOWN one index. The array will be shortened by one.

The return value is the value removed from the array.

```
my @curses = qw ( fee fie foe fum );
my $start = shift(@curses);
warn $start;
warn Dumper \@curses;
> fee
> $VAR1 = [
> 'fie',
> 'foe',
> 'fum'
> ];
```

4.5 unshift(@array, LIST)

use unshift() to add elements to the BEGINNING/BOTTOM of an array (i.e. at index ZERO). All the other elements in the array will be shifted up to make room. This will lengthen the array by the number of elements in LIST.

```
my @trees = qw ( pine maple oak );
unshift(@trees, 'birch');
warn Dumper \@trees;
> $VAR1 = [
> 'birch', # index 0
> 'pine', # old index 0, now 1
> 'maple', # 2
> 'oak' # 3
> ];
```

4.6 foreach (@array)

Use foreach to iterate through all the elements of a list. Its formal definition is:

```
LABEL foreach VAR (LIST) BLOCK
```

This is a control flow structure that is covered in more detail in the "control flow" section. The foreach structure supports last, next, and redo statements.

Use a simple foreach loop to do something to each element in an array:

```
my @fruits = qw ( apples oranges lemons pears );
foreach my $fruit (@fruits) {
   print "fruit is '$fruit'\n";
}
> fruit is 'apples'
> fruit is 'oranges'
> fruit is 'lemons'
> fruit is 'pears'
```

DO NOT ADD OR DELETE ELEMENTS TO AN ARRAY BEING PROCESSED IN A FOREACH LOOP.

```
my @numbers = qw (zero one two three);
foreach my $num (@numbers) {
   shift(@numbers) if($num eq 'one');
   print "num is '$num'\n";
}
> num is 'zero'
> num is 'one'
> num is 'three'
# note: I deleted 'zero', but I failed to
# print out 'two', which is still part of array.
# BAD!!
```

VAR acts as an alias to the element of the array itself. Changes to VAR propagate to changing the array.

```
my @integers = ( 23, 142, 9384, 83948 );
foreach my $num (@integers) {
    $num+=100;
}
print Dumper \@integers;
> $VAR1 = [
> 123,
> 242,
> 9484,
> 84048
> ];
```

4.7 sort(@array)

Use sort() to sort an array alphabetically. The return value is the sorted version of the array. The array passed in is left untouched.

```
my @fruit = qw ( pears apples bananas oranges );
my @sorted_array = sort(@fruit);
print Dumper \@sorted_array ;
>$VAR1 = [
> 'apples',
> 'bananas',
> 'oranges',
> 'pears'
> ];
```

Sorting a list of numbers will sort them alphabetically as well, which probably is not what you want.

```
my @scores = ( 1000, 13, 27, 200, 76, 150 );
my @sorted_array = sort(@scores);
print Dumper \@sorted_array ;
> $VAR1 = [
> 1000, # 1's
> 13, # 1's
> 150, # 1's
> 200,
> 27,
> 76
> ];
```

The sort() function can also take a code block (any piece of code between curly braces) which defines how to perform the sort if given any two elements from the array. The code block uses two global variables, $a and $b, and defines how to compare the two entries.

This is how you would sort an array numerically.

```
my @scores = ( 1000, 13, 27, 200, 76, 150 );
my @sorted_array = sort {$a<=>$b} (@scores);
print Dumper \@sorted_array ;

> $VAR1 = [
> 13,
> 27,
> 76,
> 150,
> 200,
> 1000
> ];
```

4.8 reverse(@array)

The reverse() function takes a list and returns an array in reverse order. The last element becomes the first element. The first element becomes the last element.

```
my @numbers = reverse (1000,13,27,200,76,150);
print Dumper \@numbers ;
> $VAR1 = [
> 150,
> 76,
> 200,
> 27,
> 13,
> 1000
> ];
```

4.9 splice(@array)

Use splice() to add or remove elements into or out of any index range of an array.

```
splice ( ARRAY , OFFSET , LENGTH , LIST );
```

The elements in ARRAY starting at OFFSET and going for LENGTH indexes will be removed from ARRAY. Any elements from LIST will be inserted at OFFSET into ARRAY.

```
my @words = qw ( hello there );
splice(@words, 1, 0, 'out');
warn join(" ", @words);

> hello out there ...
```

4.10 Undefined and Uninitialized Arrays

An array is initialized as having no entries. Therefore you can test to see if an array is initialized by calling scalar() on it. This is equivalent to calling defined() on a scalar variable. If scalar() returns false (i.e. integer 0), then the array is uninitialized.

If you want to UNintialize an array that contains data, then you do NOT want to assign it undef like you would a scalar. This would fill the array with one element at index zero with a value of undefined.

```
my @array = undef; # WRONG
```

To clear an array to its original uninitialized state, assign an empty list to it. This will clear out any entries, and leave you with a completely empty array.

```
my @array = (); # RIGHT
```

5 Hashes

Hashes are preceded with a percent sign sigil.

The "%" is a stylized "key/value" pair.

A hash stores a bunch of scalars that are accessed via a string index called a "key"

Perl hashes are ONE-DIMENSIONAL ONLY. (Do Not Panic.)

There is no order to the elements in a hash. (Well, there is, but you should not use a hash with an assumption about what order the data will come out.)

You can assign any even number of scalars to a hash. Perl will extract them in pairs. The first item will be treated as the key, and the second item will be treated as the value.

When you refer to an entire hash, use the "%" sigil.

```
my %info = qw ( name John age 42 );
```

When you look up a key in the hash, the "%" character changes to a "$" and the key is placed in curly braces.

```
my %info = qw ( name John age 42 );
my $data = $info{name};
warn $data;
> John ...
```

The keys of a hash are not pre-declared. If the key does not exist during an ASSIGNMENT, the key is created and given the assigned value.

```
my %inventory;
$inventory{apples}=42;
$inventory{pears}=17;
$inventory{bananas}=5;
print Dumper \%inventory;
>$VAR1 = {
> 'bananas' => 5,
> 'apples' => 42,
> 'pears' => 17
> };
```

If the key does not exist during a FETCH, the key is NOT created, and undef is returned.

```perl
my %inventory;
$inventory{apples}=42;
my $peaches = $inventory{peaches};
warn "peaches is '$peaches'";
print Dumper \%inventory;
> Use of uninitialized value in concatenation
> peaches is '' at ./test.pl line 13.
> $VAR1 = {
> 'apples' => 42
> };
```

5.1 exists ($hash{$key})

Use exists() to see if a key exists in a hash. You cannot simply test the value of a key, since a key might exist but store a value of FALSE

```perl
my %pets = ( cats=>2, dogs=>1 );
unless(exists($pets{fish})) {
   print "No fish here\n";
}
```

Warning: during multi-key lookup, all the lower level keys are autovivified, and only the last key has exists() tested on it. This only happens if you have a hash of hash references. References are covered later, but this is a "feature" specific to exists() that can lead to very subtle bugs. Note in the following example, we explicitly create the key "Florida", but we only test for the existence of {Maine}->{StateBird}, which has the side effect of creating the key {Maine} in the hash.

```perl
my %stateinfo;
$stateinfo{Florida}->{Abbreviation}='FL';
if (exists($stateinfo{Maine}->{StateBird})) {
   warn "it exists";
}
print Dumper \%stateinfo;

> $VAR1 = {
>           'Florida' =>    {
>                                    'Abbreviation' => 'FL'
>                            },
>           'Maine' => {}
>       };
```

You must test each level of key individually, and build your way up to the final key lookup if you do not want to autovivify the lower level keys.

```
my %stateinfo;
$stateinfo{Florida}->{Abbreviation}='FL';
if (exists($stateinfo{Maine})) {
   if (exists($stateinfo{Maine}->{StateBird}))
       { warn "it exists"; }
}
print Dumper \%stateinfo;

> $VAR1 = {
>         'Florida' =>    {
>                                 'Abbreviation' => 'FL'
>                         }
>         };
```

5.2 delete ($hash{key})

Use delete to delete a key/value pair from a hash. Once a key is created in a hash, assigning undef to it will keep the key in the hash and will only assign the value to undef.

The only way to remove a key/value pair from a hash is with delete().

```
my %pets = (
   fish=>3,
   cats=>2,
   dogs=>1,
);
$pets{cats}=undef;
delete($pets{fish});
print Dumper \%pets;

> $VAR1 = {
>           'cats' => undef,
>           'dogs' => 1
>         };
```

5.3 keys(%hash)

Use keys() to return a list of all the keys in a hash. The order of the keys will be based on the internal hashing algorithm used, and should not be something your program depends upon. Note in the example below that the order of assignment is different from the order printed out.

```
my %pets = (
    fish=>3,
    cats=>2,
    dogs=>1,
);
foreach my $pet (keys(%pets)) {
    print "pet is '$pet'\n";
}

> pet is 'cats'
> pet is 'dogs'
> pet is 'fish'
```

If the hash is very large, then you may wish to use the each() function described below.

5.4 values(%hash)

Use values() to return a list of all the values in a hash. The order of the values will match the order of the keys return in keys().

```
my %pets = (
    fish=>3,
    cats=>2,
    dogs=>1,
);
my @pet_vals = values(%pets);
print Dumper \@pet_keys;
print Dumper \@pet_vals;

> $VAR1 = [
>           2,
>           1,
>           3
>         ];
```

If the hash is very large, then you may wish to use the each() function described below.

46

5.5 each(%hash)

Use each() to iterate through each key/value pair in a hash, one at a time.

```
my %pets = (
    fish=>3,
    cats=>2,
    dogs=>1,
);
while(my($pet,$qty)=each(%pets)) {
    print "pet='$pet', qty='$qty'\n";
}

> pet='cats', qty='2'
> pet='dogs', qty='1'
> pet='fish', qty='3'
```

Every call to each() returns the next key/value pair in the hash. After the last key/value pair is returned, the next call to each() will return an empty list, which is boolean false. This is how the while loop is able to loop through each key/value and then exit when done.

Every hash has one "each iterator" attached to it. This iterator is used by perl to remember where it is in the hash for the next call to each().

Calling keys() on the hash will reset the iterator. The list returned by keys() can be discarded.

```
keys(%hash);
```

Do not add keys while iterating a hash with each().

You can delete keys while iterating a hash with each().

The each() function does not have to be used inside a while loop. This example uses a subroutine to call each() once and print out the result. The subroutine is called multiple times without using a while() loop.

```perl
my %pets = (
   fish=>3,
   cats=>2,
   dogs=>1,
);

sub one_time {
   my($pet,$qty)=each(%pets);
   # if key is not defined,
   # then each() must have hit end of hash
   if(defined($pet)) {
       print "pet='$pet', qty='$qty'\n";
   } else {
       print "end of hash\n";
   }
}

one_time; # cats
one_time; # dogs
keys(%pets); # reset the hash iterator
one_time; # cats
one_time; # dogs
one_time; # fish
one_time; # end of hash
one_time; # cats
one_time; # dogs
> pet='cats', qty='2'
> pet='dogs', qty='1'
> pet='cats', qty='2'
> pet='dogs', qty='1'
> pet='fish', qty='3'
> end of hash
> pet='cats', qty='2'
> pet='dogs', qty='1'
```

There is only one iterator variable connected with each hash, which means calling each() on a hash in a loop that then calls each() on the same hash another loop will cause problems. The example below goes through the %pets hash and attempts to compare the quantity of different pets and print out their comparison.

```perl
my %pets = (
    fish=>3,
    cats=>2,
    dogs=>1,
);
while(my($orig_pet,$orig_qty)=each(%pets)) {
    while(my($cmp_pet,$cmp_qty)=each(%pets)) {
        if($orig_qty>$cmp_qty) {
            print "there are more $orig_pet "
                ."than $cmp_pet\n";
        } else {
            print "there are less $orig_pet "
                ."than $cmp_pet\n";
        }
    }
}

> there are more cats than dogs
> there are less cats than fish
> there are more cats than dogs
> there are less cats than fish
> there are more cats than dogs
> there are less cats than fish
> there are more cats than dogs
> there are less cats than fish
> ... (stuck in an infinite loop)
```

The outside loop calls each() and gets "cats". The inside loop calls each() and gets "dogs". The inside loop continues, calls each() again, and gets "fish". The inside loop calls each() one more time and gets an empty list. The inside loop exits. The outside loop calls each() which continues where the inside loop left off, namely at the end of the list, and returns "cats". The code then enters the inside loop, and the process repeats itself indefinitely.

One solution for this each() limitation is shown below. The inner loop continues to call each() until it gets the key that matches the outer loop key. The inner loop must skip the end of the hash (an undefined key) and continue the inner loop. This also fixes a problem in the above example in that we probably do not want to compare a key to itself.

```perl
my %pets = (
    fish=>3,
    cats=>2,
    dogs=>1,
);
while(my($orig_pet,$orig_qty)=each(%pets)) {
    while(1) {
        my($cmp_pet,$cmp_qty)=each(%pets);
        next unless(defined($cmp_pet));
        last if($cmp_pet eq $orig_pet);
        if($orig_qty>$cmp_qty) {
            print "there are more $orig_pet "
                ."than $cmp_pet\n";
        } else {
            print "there are less $orig_pet "
                ."than $cmp_pet\n";
        }
    }
}

> there are more cats than dogs
> there are less cats than fish
> there are less dogs than fish
> there are less dogs than cats
> there are more fish than cats
> there are more fish than dogs
```

If you do not know the outer loop key, either because its in someone else's code and they do not pass it to you, or some similar problem, then the only other solution is to call keys on the hash for all inner loops, store the keys in an array, and loop through the array of keys using foreach. The inner loop will then not rely on the internal hash iterator value.

6 List Context

List context is a concept built into the grammar of perl. You cannot declare a "list context" in perl the way you might declare an @array or %hash. List context affects how perl executes your source code. Here is an example.

```
my @cart1=qw( milk bread butter);
my @cart2=qw( eggs bacon juice );
my @checkout_counter = ( @cart1, @cart2 );
print Dumper \@checkout_counter;

> $VAR1 = [
>     'milk',
>     'bread',
>     'butter',
>     'eggs',
>     'bacon',
>     'juice'
> ];
```

Basically, two people with grocery carts, @cart1 and @cart2, pulled up to the @checkout_counter and unloaded their carts without putting one of those separator bars in between them. The person behind the @checkout_counter has no idea whose groceries are whose.

Everything in list context gets reduced to an ordered series of scalars. The original container that held the scalars is forgotten.

In the above example the order of scalars is retained: milk, bread, butter is the order of scalars in @cart1 and the order of the scalars at the beginning of @checkout_counter. However, looking at just @checkout_counter, there is no way to know where the contents of @cart1 end and the contents of @cart2 begin. In fact, @cart1 might have been empty, and all the contents of @checkout_counter could belong to @cart2, but there is no way to know.

Sometimes, list context can be extremely handy. We have used list context repeatedly to initialize arrays and hashes and it worked as we would intuitively expect:

```
my %pets = ( fish=>3, cats=>2, dogs=>1 );
my @cart1 = qw( milk bread eggs);
```

The initial values for the hash get converted into an ordered list of scalars

```
( 'fish', 3, 'cats', 2, 'dogs', 1 )
```

These scalars are then used in list context to initialize the hash, using the first scalar as a key and the following scalar as its value, and so on throughout the list.

List context applies anytime data is passed around in perl. Scalars, arrays, and hashes are all affected by list context. In the example below, @house is intended to contain a list of all the items in the house. However, because the %pets hash was reduced to scalars in list context, the values 3,2,1 are disassociated from their keys. The @house variable is not very useful.

```
my %pets = ( fish=>3, cats=>2, dogs=>1 );
my @refrigerator=qw(milk bread eggs);
my @house=('couch',%pets,@refrigerator,'chair');
print Dumper \@house;
>$VAR1 = [
>       'couch',
>       'cats',
>       2,
>       'dogs',
>       1,
>       'fish',
>       3,
>       'milk',
>       'bread',
>       'eggs',
>       'chair'
> ];
```

There are times when list context on a hash does make sense.

```
my %encrypt=(tank=>'turtle',bomber=>'eagle');
my %decrypt=reverse(%encrypt) ;
print Dumper \%decrypt;
> $VAR1 = {
>       'eagle' => 'bomber',
>       'turtle' => 'tank'
> };
```

The %encrypt hash contains a hash look up to encrypt plaintext into cyphertext. Anytime you want to use the word "bomber", you actually send the word "eagle". The decryption is the opposite. Anytime you receive the word "eagle" you need to translate that to the word "bomber".

Using the %encrypt hash to perform decryption would require a loop that called each() on the %encrypt hash, looping until it found the value that matched the word received over the radio. This could take too long.

Instead, because there is no overlap between keys and values, (two different words don't encrypt to the same word), we can simply treat the %encrypt hash as a list, call the array reverse() function on it, which flips the list around from end to end, and then store that reversed list into a %decrypt hash.

7 References

References are a thing that refer (point) to something else.

The "something else" is called the "referent", the thing being pointed to.

Taking a reference and using it to access the referent is called "dereferencing".

A good real-world example is a driver's license. Your license "points" to where you live because it lists your home address. Your license is a "reference". The "referent" is your home. And if you have forgotten where you live, you can take your license and "dereferencing" it to get yourself home.

It is possible that you have roommates, which would mean multiple references exist to point to the same home. But there can only be one home per address.

In perl, references are stored in scalars. You can create a reference by creating some data (scalar, array, hash) and putting a "\" in front of it.

```perl
my %home= (
    fish=>3,cats=>2,dogs=>1,
    milk=>1,bread=>2,eggs=>12,
);
my $license_for_alice = \%home;
my $license_for_bob   = \%home;
```

Alice and Bob are roommates and their licenses are references to the same %home. This means that Alice could bring in a bunch of new pets and Bob could eat the bread out of the refrigerator even though Alice might have been the one to put it there. To do this, Alice and Bob need to dereference their licenses and get into the original %home hash.

```perl
$ {$license_for_alice} {dogs} += 5;
delete($ {$license_for_bob} {milk});
print Dumper \%home;
> $VAR1 = {
>     'eggs' => 12,
>     'cats' => 2,
>     'bread' => 2,
>     'dogs' => 6,
>     'fish' => 3
> };
```

7.1 Named Referents

A referent is any original data structure: a scalar, array, or hash. Below, we declare some named referents: age, colors, and pets.

```
my $age = 42;
my @colors = qw( red green blue );
my %pets=(fish=>3,cats=>2,dogs=>1);
```

7.2 References to Named Referents

A reference points to the referent. To take a reference to a named referent, put a "\" in front of the named referent.

```
my $ref_to_age = \$age;
my $r_2_colors = \@colors;
my $r_pets = \%pets;
```

7.3 Dereferencing

To dereference, place the reference in curly braces and prefix it with the sigil of the appropriate type. This will give access to the entire original referent.

```
${$ref_to_age}++; # happy birthday
pop(@{$r_2_colors});
my %copy_of_pets = %{$r_pets};
print "age is '$age'\n";
> age is '43'
```

If there is no ambiguity in dereferencing, the curly braces are not needed.

```
$$ref_to_age ++; # another birthday
print "age is '$age'\n";
> age is '44'
```

It is also possible to dereference into an array or hash with a specific index or key.

```perl
my @colors = qw( red green blue );
my %pets=(fish=>3,cats=>2,dogs=>1);
my $r_colors = \@colors; my $r_pets = \%pets;
${$r_pets}{dogs} += 5;
${$r_colors}[1] = 'yellow';
print Dumper \@colors; print Dumper \%pets;
> $VAR1 = [
'red',
'yellow', # green turned to yellow
'blue'
];
$VAR1 = {
'cats' => 2,
'dogs' => 6, # 5 new dogs
'fish' => 3
};
```

Because array and hash referents are so common, perl has a shorthand notation for indexing into an array or looking up a key in a hash using a reference. Take the reference, follow it by "->", and then follow that by either "[index]" or "{key}". This:

```perl
${$r_pets}{dogs} += 5;
${$r_colors}[1] = 'yellow';
```

is exactly the same as this:

```perl
$r_pets->{dogs} += 5;
$r_colors->[1] = 'yellow';
```

7.4 Anonymous Referents

Here are some referents named age, colors, and pets. Each named referent has a reference to it as well.

```
my $age = 42;
my @colors = qw( red green blue );
my %pets=(fish=>3,cats=>2,dogs=>1);
my $r_age = \$age;
my $r_colors = \@colors;
my $r_pets = \%pets;
```

It is also possible in perl to create an ANONYMOUS REFERENT. An anonymous referent has no name for the underlying data structure and can only be accessed through the reference.

To create an anonymous array referent, put the contents of the array in square brackets.

The square brackets will create the underlying array with no name, and return a reference to that unnamed array.

```
my $colors_ref = [ 'red', 'green', 'blue' ];
print Dumper $colors_ref;
> $VAR1 = [
>     'red',
>     'green',
>     'blue'
> ];
```

To create an anonymous hash referent, put the contents of the hash in curly braces. The curly braces will create the underlying hash with no name, and return a reference to that unnamed hash.

```
my $pets_ref = { fish=>3,cats=>2,dogs=>1 };
print Dumper $pets_ref;
> $VAR1 = {
> 'cats' => 2,
> 'dogs' => 1,
> 'fish' => 3
> };
```

Note that $colors_ref is a reference to an array, but that array has no name to directly access its data. You must use $colors_ref to access the data in the array. Likewise, $pets_ref is a reference to a hash, but that hash has no name to directly access its data. You must use $pets_ref to access the data in the hash.

7.5 Complex Data Structures

Arrays and hashes can only store scalar values. But because scalars can hold references, complex data structures are now possible. Using references is one way to avoid the problems associated with list context. Here is another look at the house example, but now using references.

```
my %pets = ( fish=>3, cats=>2, dogs=>1 );
my @refrigerator=qw(milk bread eggs);
my $house={
      pets=>\%pets,
      refrigerator=>\@refrigerator
};
print Dumper $house;
> $VAR1 = {
>     'pets' => {
>        'cats' => 2,
>        'dogs' => 1,
>        'fish' => 3
>     },
>     'refrigerator' => [
>        'milk',
>        'bread',
>        'eggs'
>     ]
> };
```

The $house variable is a reference to an anonymous hash, which contains two keys, "pets" and "refrigerator". These keys are associated with values that are references as well, one a hash reference and the other an array reference.

Dereferencing a complex data structure can be done with the arrow notation or by enclosing the reference in curly braces and prefixing it with the appropriate sigil.

```
# Alice added more canines
$house->{pets}->{dogs}+=5;
# Bob drank all the milk
shift(@{$house->{refrigerator}});
```

7.5.1 Autovivification

Perl autovivifies any structure needed when assigning or fetching from a reference. The autovivified referents are anonymous. Perl will assume you know what you are doing with your structures. In the example below, we start out with an undefined scalar called $scal. We then fetch from this undefined scalar, as if it were a reference to an array of a hash of an array of a hash of an array. Perl autovivifies everything under the assumption that that is what you wanted to do.

```
my $scal;
my $val =
$scal->[2]->{somekey}->[1]->{otherkey}->[1];
print Dumper $scal;
> $VAR1 = [
>     undef,
>     ${\$VAR1->[0]},
>     {
>         'somekey' => [
>             ${\$VAR1->[0]},
>             {
>                 'otherkey' => []
>             }
>         ]
>     }
> ];
```

If this is NOT what you want to do, check for the existence of each hash key and check that the array contains at least enough array entries to handle the given index.

7.5.2 Multidimensional Arrays

Perl implements multidimensional arrays using one-dimensional arrays and references.

```perl
my $mda;
for(my $i=0;$i<2;$i++){
    for(my $j=0;$j<2;$j++) {
        for(my $k=0;$k<2;$k++){
            $mda->[$i]->[$j]->[$k] =
                "row=$i, col=$j, depth=$k";
        }
    }
}
print Dumper $mda;
> $VAR1 = [
>           [
>             [
>               'row=0, col=0, depth=0',
>               'row=0, col=0, depth=1'
>             ],
>             [
>               'row=0, col=1, depth=0',
>               'row=0, col=1, depth=1'
>             ]
>           ],
>           [
>             [
>               'row=1, col=0, depth=0',
>               'row=1, col=0, depth=1'
>             ],
>             [
>               'row=1, col=1, depth=0',
>               'row=1, col=1, depth=1'
>             ]
>           ]
>         ];
```

7.5.3 Deep Cloning, Deep Copy

If you need to create an entirely separate but identical clone of a complex data structure, use the Storable.pm perl module. Storable comes standard with perl 5.8. If you don't have 5.8 installed, consider an upgrade. Otherwise, read the section about CPAN later in this document, download Storable from CPAN, and install.

Then use Storable in your perl code, indicating you want to import the 'nstore', 'dclone', and 'retrieve' subroutines. The 'use' statement is explained later in this document as well, for now, it isn't that important.

The 'dclone' subroutine takes a reference to any kind of data structure and returns a reference to a deep cloned version of that data structure.

```
use Storable qw(nstore dclone retrieve);
my $scal;
$scal->[2]->{somekey}->[1]->{otherkey}->[1];
# $twin is an identical clone of $scal
my $twin = dclone $scal;
```

7.6 Data Persistence

The Storable.pm module also contains two subroutines for storing the contents of any perl data structure to a file and retrieving it later.

```
use Storable qw(nstore dclone retrieve);
my $scal;
$scal->[2]->{somekey}->[1]->{otherkey}->[1];
nstore ($scal, 'filename');
# exit, reboot computer, and restart script
my $revived = retrieve('filename');
```

7.7 Stringification of References

Perl will stringify a reference if you try to do anything string-like with it, such as print it.

```
my $referent = 42;
my $reference = \$referent;
warn "reference is '$reference'";
> reference is 'SCALAR(0x812e6ec)' ...
```

But perl will not allow you to create a string and attempt to turn it into a reference.

```perl
my $reference = 'SCALAR(0x812e6ec)';
my $value = $$reference;
> Can't use string ("SCALAR(0x812e6ec)") as
> a SCALAR ref while "strict refs" in use
```

Turning strict off only gives you undef.

```perl
no strict;
my $reference = 'SCALAR(0x812e6ec)';
my $value = $$reference;
warn "value not defined" unless(defined($value));
warn "value is '$value'\n";
> value not defined
> Use of uninitialized value in concatenation
```

Because a reference is always a string that looks something like "SCALAR(0x812e6ec)", it will evaluate true when treated as a boolean, even if the value to which it points is false.

7.8 The ref() function

The ref() function takes a scalar and returns a string indicating what kind of referent the scalar is referencing. If the scalar is not a reference, ref() returns false (an empty string).

```
my $temp = \42;
my $string = ref($temp);
warn "string is '$string'";
> string is 'SCALAR'
```

Here we call ref() on several types of variable:

```
sub what_is_it {
    my ($scalar)=@_;
    my $string = ref($scalar);
    print "string is '$string'\n";
}
what_is_it( \'hello' );
what_is_it( [1,2,3] );
what_is_it( {cats=>2} );
what_is_it( 42 );
> string is 'SCALAR'
> string is 'ARRAY'
> string is 'HASH'
> string is ''
```

Note that this is like stringification of a reference except without the address being part of the string. Instead of SCALAR(0x812e6ec), its just SCALAR. Also note that if you stringify a non-reference, you get the scalar value. But if you call ref() on a nonreference, you get an empty string, which is always false.

8 Control Flow

Standard statements get executed in sequential order in perl.

```perl
my $name = 'John Smith';
my $greeting = "Hello, $name\n";
print $greeting;
```

Control flow statements allow you to alter the order of execution while the program is running.

```perl
if( $price == 0 ) {
    print "Free Beer!\n";
}
```

Perl supports the following control flow structures:

```
##
LABEL is an optional name that identifies the
# control flow structure.
# It is a bareword identifier followed by a colon.
# example==> MY_NAME:
##
SINGLE_STATEMENT ==> a single perl statement
# NOT including the semicolon.
# print "hello\n"
##
BLOCK ==> zero or more statements contained
# in curly braces { print "hi"; }
LABEL BLOCK
LABEL BLOCK continue BLOCK
# BOOL ==> boolean (see boolean section above)
SINGLE_STATEMENT if (BOOL);if (BOOL) BLOCK
if (BOOL) BLOCK else BLOCK
if (BOOL) BLOCK elsif (BOOL) BLOCK elsif ()...
if (BOOL) BLOCK elsif (BOOL) BLOCK ... else BLOCKunless (BOOL) BLOCK
unless (BOOL) BLOCK else BLOCK
unless (BOOL) BLOCK elsif (BOOL) BLOCK elsif ()...
unless (BOOL) BLOCK elsif (BOOL) BLOCK ... else BLOCK
LABEL while (BOOL) BLOCK
LABEL while (BOOL) BLOCK continue BLOCK
LABEL until (BOOL) BLOCK
LABEL until (BOOL) BLOCK continue BLOCK
# INIT, TEST, CONT are all expressions
# INIT is an initialization expression
# INIT is evaluated once prior to loop entry
# TEST is BOOLEAN expression that controls loop exit
# TEST is evaluated each time after
# BLOCK is executed
# CONT is a continuation expression
# CONT is evaluated each time TEST is evaluated TRUE
LABEL for ( INIT; TEST; CONT ) BLOCK
# LIST is a list of scalars, see arrays and
# list context sections later in text
LABEL foreach (LIST) BLOCK
LABEL foreach VAR (LIST) BLOCK
LABEL foreach VAR (LIST) BLOCK continue BLOCK
```

8.1 Labels

Labels are always optional. A label is an identifier followed by a colon.

A label is used to give its associated control flow structure a name.

Inside a BLOCK of a control flow structure, you can call

```
next;
last;
redo;
```

If the structure has a LABEL, you can call

```
next LABEL;
last LABEL;
redo LABEL;
```

If no label is given to next, last, or redo, then the command will operate on the inner-most control structure. If a label is given, then the command will operate on the control structure given.

8.2 last LABEL;

The last command goes to the end of the entire control structure. It does not execute any continue block if one exists.

8.3 next LABEL;

The next command skips the remaining BLOCK. if there is a continue block, execution resumes there. After the continue block finishes, or if no continue block exists, execution starts the next iteration of the control construct if it is a loop construct.

8.4 redo LABEL;

The redo command skips the remaining BLOCK. It does not execute any continue block (even if it exists). Execution then resumes at the start of the control structure without evaluating the conditional again.

9 Packages and Namespaces and Lexical Scoping

9.1 Package Declaration

Perl has a package declaration statement that looks like this:

```
package NAMESPACE;
```

This package declaration indicates that the rest of the enclosing block, subroutine, eval, or file belongs to the namespace given by NAMESPACE.

The standard warnings, strictness, and Data::Dumper are attached to the namespace in which they were turned on with "use warnings;" etc. Anytime you declare a new package namespace, you will want to "use" these again.

```
package SomeOtherPackage;
use warnings; use strict; use Data::Dumper;
```

All perl scripts start with an implied declaration of:

```
package main;
```

You can access package variables with the appropriate sigil, followed by the package name, followed by a double colon, followed by the variable name. This is called a package QUALIFIED variable meaning the package name is explicitly stated.

```
$package_this::age;
@other_package::refrigerator;
%package_that::pets;
```

If you use an UNQUALIFIED variable in your code, perl assumes it is in the the most recently declared package namespace that was declared.

When you have strict-ness turned on, there are two ways to create and use package variables:

1) Use the fully package qualified name everywhere in your code:

```
# can use variable without declaring it with 'my'
$some_package::answer=42;
warn "The value is '$some_package::answer'\n"
```

9.2 Declaring Package Variables With our

2) Use "our" to declare the variable.

```
package this_package;
our $name='John';
warn "name is '$name'";
```

Using "our" is the preferred method. You must have perl 5.6.0 or later for "our" declarations.

The difference between the two methods is that always using package qualified variable names means you do NOT have to declare the package you are in. You can create variables in ANY namespace you want, without ever having to declare the namespace explicitly. You can even declare variables in someone else's package namespace. There is no restrictions in perl that prevent you from doing this.

To encourage programmers to play nice with each other's namespaces, the "our" function was created. Declaring a variable with "our" will create the variable in the current namespace. If the namespace is other than "main", then you will need to declare the package namespace explicitly. However, once a package variable is declared with "our", the fully package qualified name is NOT required, and you can refer to the variable just on its variable name, as example (2) above refers to the $name package variable.

We do not HAVE to use the "our" shortcut even if we used it to declare it. The "our" declaration is a shorthand for declaring a package variable. Once the package variable exists, we can access it any way we wish.

```
package Hogs;
our $speak = 'oink';
warn "Hogs::speak is '$Hogs::speak'";
> Hogs::speak is 'oink' ...
```

9.3 Package Variables inside a Lexical Scope

When you declare a package inside a code block, that package namespace declaration remains in effect until the end of the block, at which time, the package namespace reverts to the previous namespace.

```
package Hogs;
our $speak = 'oink';
{ # START OF CODE BLOCK
   package Heifers;
   our $speak = 'moo';
} # END OF CODE BLOCK
warn "speak is '$speak'";
> speak is 'oink' ...
```

The Heifers namespace still exists, as does all the variables that were declared in that namespace. Its just that outside the code block, the "our Heifers;" declaration has worn off, and we now have to use a fully package qualified name to get to the variables in Heifers package. This "wearing off" is a function of the code block being a "lexical scope" and a package declaration only lasts to the end of the current lexical scope. The package variables declared inside the code block "survive" after the code block ends.

```
{
package Heifers;
our $speak = 'moo';
}
print "Heifers::speak is '$Heifers::speak'\n";
> Heifers::speak is 'moo'
```

9.4 Lexical Scope

Lexical refers to words or text. A lexical scope exists while execution takes place inside of a particular chunk of source code. In the above examples, the "package Heifers;" only exists inside the curly braces of the source code. Outside those curly braces, the package declaration has gone out of scope, which is a technical way of saying its "worn off". Scope refers to vision, as in telescope. Within a lexical scope, things that have lexical limitations (such as a package declaration) are only "visible" inside that lexical space.

So "lexical scope" refers to anything that is visible or has an effect only withing a certain boundary of the source text or source code. The easiest way to demonstrate lexical scoping is lexical variables, and to show how lexical variables differ from "our" variables.

9.5 Lexical Variables

Lexical variables are declared with the `my` keyword. Lexical variables declared inside a lexical scope do not survive outside the lexical scope.

```
no warnings;
no strict;
{
    my $speak = 'moo';
}
warn "speak is '$speak'\n";
> speak is ''
```

The lexical variable "$speak" goes out of scope at the end of the code block (at the "}" character), so it does not exist when we try to print it out after the block. We had to turn warnings and strict off just to get it to compile because with warnings and strict on, perl will know $speak does not exist when you attempt to print it, so it will throw an exception and quit.

Lexically scoped variables have three main features:

1) Lexical variables do not belong to any package namespace, so you cannot prefix them with a package name. The example below shows that `my $cnt` is not the same as the `main::cnt`

```
no warnings;
package main;
my $cnt='I am just a lexical';
warn "main::cnt is '$main::cnt'";
> main::cnt is ''
```
2) Lexical variables are only directly accessible from the point where they are declared to the end of the nearest enclosing block, subroutine, eval, or file.

```
no strict;
{
    my $some_lex = 'I am lex';
}
warn "some_lex is '$some_lex'";
> some_lex is ''
```

3) Lexical variables are subject to "garbage collection" at the end of scope. If nothing is using a lexical variable at the end of scope, perl will remove it from its memory. Every time a variable is declared with "my", it is created dynamically, during execution. The location of the variable will change each time. Note in the example below, we create a new $lex_var each time through the loop, and $lex_var is at a different address each time.

```
my @cupboard;
for (1 .. 5) {
   my $lex_var ='canned goods';
   my $lex_ref = \$lex_var;
   push(@cupboard, $lex_ref);
   print "$lex_ref\n";
}
> SCALAR(0x812e770)
> SCALAR(0x812e6c8)
> SCALAR(0x812e6e0)
> SCALAR(0x81624c8)
> SCALAR(0x814cf64)
```

Lexical variables are just plain good. They generally keep you from stepping on someone else's toes. They also keep your data more private than a package variable. Package variables are permanent, never go out of scope, never get garbage collected, and are accessible from anyone's script.

9.6 Garbage Collection

When a lexical variable goes out of scope, perl will check to see if anyone is using that variable, and if no one is using it, perl will delete that variable and free up memory.

The freed up memory is not returned to the system, rather the freed up memory is used for possible declarations of new lexically scoped variables that could be declared later in the program.

This means that your program will never get smaller because of lexical variables going out of scope. Once the memory is allocated for perl, it remains under perl's jurisdiction. But perl can use garbage collected space for other lexical variables.

If a lexical variable is a referent of another variable, then the lexical will not be garbage collected when it goes out of scope.

```
no strict;
my $referring_var;
{
   my $some_lex = 'I am lex';
   $referring_var=\$some_lex;
}
warn "some_lex is '$some_lex'";
warn "referring var refers to '$$referring_var'";
> some_lex is ''
> referring var refers to 'I am lex'
```

When the lexical $some_lex went out of scope, we could no longer access it directly. But since $referring_var is a reference to $some_lex, then $some_lex was never garbage collected, and it retained its value of "I am lex". The data in $some_lex was still accessible through referring_var.

Note that the named variable $some_lex went out of scope at the end of the code block and could not be accessed by name.

9.6.1 Reference Count Garbage Collection

Perl uses reference count based garbage collection. It is rudimentary reference counting, so circular references will not get collected even if nothing points to the circle. The example below shows two variables that refer to each other but nothing refers to the two variables. Perl will not garbage collect these variables even though they are completely inaccessible by the end of the code block.

```
{
my ($first,$last);
($first,$last)=(\$last,\$first);
}
```

9.6.2 Garbage Collection and Subroutines

Garbage collection does not rely strictly on references to a variable to determine if it should be garbage collected. If a subroutine uses a lexical variable, then that variable will not be garbage collected as long as the subroutine exists.

Subroutines that use a lexical variable declared outside of the subroutine declaration are called "CLOSURES".

In the example below, the lexical variable, $cnt, is declared inside a code block and would normally get garbage collected at the end of the block. However, two subroutines are declared in that same code block that use $cnt, so $cnt is not garbage collected. Since $cnt goes out of scope, the only things that can access it after the code block are the subroutines. Note that a reference to $cnt is never taken, however perl knows that $cnt is needed by the subroutines and therefore keeps it around. The inc and dec subroutines are subroutine closures.

```
{   my $cnt=0;
    sub inc{$cnt++; print "cnt is '$cnt'\n";}
    sub dec{$cnt--; print "cnt is '$cnt'\n";}
}
inc;
inc;
inc;
dec;
> cnt is '1'
> cnt is '2'
> cnt is '3'
> cnt is '2'
```

Subroutine names are like names of package variables. The subroutine gets placed in the current declared package namespace. Therefore, named subroutines are like package variables in that, once declared, they never go out of scope or get garbage collected.

9.7 Package Variables Revisited

Package variables are not evil, they are just global variables, and they inherit all the possible problems associated with using global variables in your code. In the event you DO end up using a package variable in your code, they do have some advantages. They are global, which means they can be a convenient way for several different blocks of perl code to talk amongst themselves using an agreed upon global variable as their channel.

Imagine several subroutines across several files that all want to check a global variable: $Development::Verbose. If this variable is true, these subroutines print detailed information. If it is false, these subroutines print little or no information.

```
package Development;
our $Verbose=1;
sub Compile {
if ($Development::Verbose) {
   print "compiling\n"; }
}
sub Link {
   if ($Development::Verbose){
      print "linking\n";
   }
}
sub Run {
   if ($Development::Verbose){
      print "running\n";
   }
}
Compile;
Link;
Run;
> compiling
> linking
> running
```

The three subroutines could be in different files, in different package namespaces, and they could all access the $Development::Verbose variable and act accordingly.

9.8 Calling local() on Package Variables

When working with global variables, there are times when you want to save the current value of the global variable, set it to a new and temporary value, execute some foreign code that will access this global, and then set the global back to what it was.

Continuing the previous example, say we wish to create a RunSilent subroutine that stores $Development::Verbose in a temp variable, calls the original Run routine, and then sets $Development::Verbose back to its original value.

```perl
package Development;
our $Verbose=1;
sub Compile {
   if ($Development::Verbose) {
      print "compiling\n";
   }
}
sub Link {
   if ($Development::Verbose){
      print "linking\n";
   }
}
sub Run {
   if ($Development::Verbose){
      print "running\n";
   }
}
sub RunSilent {
   my $temp = $Development::Verbose;
   $Development::Verbose=0;
   Run;
   $Development::Verbose=$temp;
}
Compile;
Link;
RunSilent;
> compiling
> linking
```

This can also be accomplished with the "local()" function. The local function takes a package variable, saves off the original value, allows you to assign a temp value to it. That new value is seen by anyone accessing the variable. And at the end of the lexical scope in which local() was called, the original value for the variable is returned. The RunSilent subroutine could be written like this:

```
sub RunSilent {
    local($Development::Verbose)=0;
    Run;
}
```

Perl originally started with nothing but package variables. The "my" lexical variables were not introduced until perl version 4. So to deal with all the package variables, perl was given the local() function. Local is also a good way to create a temporary variable and make sure you don't step on someone else's variable of the same name.

10 Subroutines

Perl allows you to declare named subroutines and anonymous subroutines, similar to the way you can declare named variables and anonymous variables.

10.1 Subroutine Sigil

Subroutines use the ampersand (&) as their sigil. But while the sigils for scalars, arrays, and hashes are mandatory, the sigil for subroutines is optional.
1.1Named Subroutines
Below is the named subroutine declaration syntax:

```
sub NAME BLOCK
```

NAME can be any valid perl identifier.

BLOCK is a code block enclosed in parenthesis.

The NAME of the subroutine is placed in the current package namespace, in the same way "our" variables go into the current package namespace. So once a named subroutine is declared, you may access it with just NAME if you are in the correct package, or with a fully package qualified name if you are outside the package. And you can use the optional ampersand sigil in either case.

```
package MyArea;
sub Ping {print "ping\n";}
Ping;
&Ping;
MyArea::Ping;
&MyArea::Ping;
> ping
> ping
> ping
> ping
```

Once the current package declaration changes, you MUST use a fully package qualified subroutine name to call the subroutine.

```
package MyArea;
sub Ping {print "ping\n";}
package YourArea;
MyArea::Ping;
&MyArea::Ping;
&Ping; # error, looking in current package YourArea
> ping
> ping
> Undefined subroutine &YourArea::Ping
```

10.2 Anonymous Subroutines

Below is the anonymous subroutine declaration syntax:

```
sub BLOCK
```

This will return a code reference, similar to how [] returns an array reference, and similar to how {} returns a hash reference.

```
sub what_is_it {
   my ($scalar)=@_;
   my $string = ref($scalar);
   print "ref returned '$string'\n";
}
my $temp = sub {print "Hello\n";};
what_is_it($temp);
> ref returned 'CODE'
```

10.3 Data::Dumper and subroutines

The contents of the code block are invisible to anything outside the code block. For this reason, things like Data::Dumper cannot look inside the code block and show you the actual code. Instead Data::Dumper does not even try and just gives you a place holder that returns a dummy string.

```
my $temp = sub {print "Hello\n";};
print Dumper $temp;
> $VAR1 = sub { "DUMMY" };
```

10.4 Passing Arguments to/from a Subroutine

Any values you want to pass to a subroutine get put in the parenthesis at the subroutine call. For normal subroutines, all arguments go through the list context crushing machine and get reduced to a list of scalars. The original containers are not known inside the subroutine. The subroutine will not know if the list of scalars it receives came from scalars, arrays, or hashes. To avoid some of the list context crushing, a subroutine can be declared with a prototype, which are discussed later.

10.5 Accessing Arguments inside Subroutines via @_

Inside the subroutine, the arguments are accessed via a special array called @_, since all the arguments passed in were reduced to list context, these arguments fit nicely into an array. The @_ array can be processed just like any other regular array. If the arguments are fixed and known, the preferred way to extract them is to assign @_ to a list of scalars with meaningful names.

```perl
sub compare {
    my ($left,$right)=@_;
    return $left<=>$right;
}
```

The @_ array is "magical" in that it is really a list of aliases for the original arguments passed in. Therefore, assigning a value to an element in @_ will change the value in the original variable that was passed into the subroutine call.

Subroutine parameters are effectively IN/OUT.

```perl
sub swap { (@_) = reverse(@_); }
my $one = "I am one";
my $two = "I am two";
swap($one,$two);
warn "one is '$one'";
warn "two is '$two'";
> one is 'I am two'
> two is 'I am one'
```

Assigning to the entire @_ array does not work, you have to assign to the individual elements. If swap were defined like this, the variables $one and $two would remain unchanged.

```perl
sub swap {
    my ($left,$right)=@_;
    @_ = ($right,$left);  #WRONG
}
```

10.6 Dereferencing Code References

Dereferencing a code reference causes the subroutine to be called. A code reference can be dereferenced by preceding it with an ampersand sigil or by using the arrow operator and parenthesis "->()". The preferred way is to use the arrow operator with parens.

```
my $temp = sub {print "Hello\n";};
&{$temp};
&$temp;
$temp->(); # preferred
> Hello
> Hello
> Hello
```

10.7 Implied Arguments

When calling a subroutine with the "&" sigil prefix and no parenthesis, the current @_ array gets implicitly passed to the subroutine being called. This can cause subtly odd behavior if you are not expecting it.

```
sub second_level {
    print Dumper \@_;
}

sub first_level {
    # using '&' sigil and no parens.
    # doesn't look like I'm passing any params
    # but perl will pass @_ implicitly.
    &second_level;
}

first_level(1,2,3);
> $VAR1 = [
> 1,
> 2,
> 3
> ];
```

This generally is not a problem with named subroutines because you probably will not use the "&" sigil. However, when using code references, dereferencing using the "&" may cause implied arguments to be passed to the new subroutine. For this reason, the arrow operator is the preferred way to dereference a code reference.

```
$code_ref->(); # pass nothing, no implicit @_
$code_ref->(@_); # explicitly pass @_
$code_ref->( 'one', 'two' ); # pass new parameters
```

10.8 Subroutine Return Value

Subroutines can return a single value or a list of values. The return value can be explicit, or it can be implied to be the last statement of the subroutine. An explicit return statement is the preferred approach if any return value is desired.

```
# return a single scalar
sub ret_scal {
    return "boo";
}
my $scal_var = ret_scal;
print Dumper \$scal_var;
# return a list of values
sub ret_arr {
    return (1,2,3);
}
my @arr_var =ret_arr;
print Dumper \@arr_var;
> $VAR1 = \'boo';
> $VAR1 = [
>  1,
>  2,
>  3
> ];
```

10.9 Returning False

The return value of a subroutine is often used within a boolean test. The problem is that the subroutine needs to know if it is called in scalar context or array context.

Returning a simple "undef" value (or 0 or 0.0 or "") will work in scalar context, but in array context, it will create an array with the first element set to undef. In boolean context, an array with one or more elements is considered true.

A return statement by itself will return undef in scalar context and an empty list in list context. This is the preferred way to return false in a subroutine.

```
sub this_is_false {
    return; # undef or empty list
}
my $scal_var = this_is_false;
my @arr_var = this_is_false;
print Dumper \$scal_var;
print Dumper \@arr_var;

> $VAR1 = \undef;  <== return to a scalar returns undef
> $VAR1 = [];      <== return to an array returns empty array
```

To explicitly return based on what the return context is, use the caller() function, index [5] of its return value, which indicates whether the caller wants a return value in an array context or not (scalar).

```
return wantarray() ? () : 0; # FALSE
```

10.10 Using the caller() Function in Subroutines

The caller() function can be used in a subroutine to find out information about where the subroutine was called from and how it was called. Caller takes one argument that indicates how far back in the call stack to get its information from. For information about the current subroutine, use caller(0).

```
sub HowWasICalled {
    my @info = caller(0);
    print Dumper \@info;
}
HowWasICalled;
>$VAR1 = [
> 'main',
> './test.pl',
> 13,
> 'main::HowWasICalled',
> 1,
> undef,
> undef,
> undef,
> 2,
> 'UUUUUUUUUUUU'
> ];
```

The caller() function returns a list of information in the following order

```
0 $package   package namespace at time of call
1 $filename  filename where called occurred
2 $line      line number in file where call occurred
3 $subroutine name of subroutine called
4 $hasargs   true if explicit arguments passed in
5 $wantarray list=1, scalar=0, void=undef
6 $evaltext  evaluated text if an eval block
7 $is_require true if created by "require" or "use"
8 $hints     internal use only, disregard
9 $bitmask   internal use only, disregard
```

Note in the example above, the code is in a file called test.pl. The call occurred in package main, the default package namespace, and it occurred at line 13 of the file. The package qualified name of the subroutine that was called was main::HowWasICalled. The package qualified name must be given since you don't know what package is current where the subroutine was called from, that information is hidden in lexical scope.

10.11 The wantarray() function

The wantarray() function returns the same value found in the caller(0) return value, index [5]. This indicates what return value is expected of the subroutine from where it was called. The subroutine could have been called in void context meaning the return value is thrown away. Or it could have been called and the return value assigned to a scalar. Or it could have been called and the return value assigned to a list of scalars.

```perl
sub CheckMyWantArray {
   my $wantarray=defined(wantarray())?wantarray():'undef';
   print "wantarray is '$wantarray' \n";
}

# first call has no return value, wantarray() is undef.
CheckMyWantArray;                   # undef          (FALSE)
my $scal = CheckMyWantArray;        # empty string   (FALSE)
my @arr  = CheckMyWantArray;        # 1              (TRUE)
> wantarray is 'undef'
> wantarray is ''
> wantarray is '1'
```

10.12 Context Sensitive Subroutines with wantarray()

You can use the wantarray() function to create a subroutine that is sensitive to the context in which it was called.

```perl
sub ArrayProcessor {
   if(wantarray()) {
      return (@_);          # return the array passed in
   } else {
      return scalar(@_);    # return size of array passed in
   }
}
my @arr=qw(alpha bravo charlie);
ArrayProcessor(@arr);
my $scal = ArrayProcessor(@arr); # 3
my @ret_arr = ArrayProcessor(@arr); # alpha ...
print "scal is '$scal'\nret_arr is " . (Dumper \@ret_arr);
> scal is '3'

> ret_arr is $VAR1 = [
>           'alpha',
>           'bravo',
>           'charlie'
>         ];
```

11 Compiling and Interpreting

When perl works on your source code, it will always be in one of two modes: compiling or interpreting. Perl has some hooks to allow access into these different cycles. They are code blocks that are prefixed with BEGIN, CHECK, INIT, and END.

Compiling: translating the source text into machine usable internal format.

Interpreting: executing the machine usable, internal format.

The BEGIN block is immediate.

BEGIN -> interpret block as soon as it is compiled, even before compiling anything else.

The other blocks, including normal code, do not execute until after the entire program has been compiled. When anything other than a BEGIN block is encountered, they are compiled and scheduled for execution, but perl continues compiling the rest of the program.

The execution order is BEGIN, CHECK, INIT, normal code, and END blocks.

CHECK -> Schedule these blocks for execution after all source code has been compiled.

INIT -> Schedule these blocks for execution after the CHECK blocks have executed.

normal code -> Schedule normal code to execute after all INIT blocks.

END -> Schedule for execution after normal code has completed.

Multiple BEGIN blocks are executed immediately in NORMAL declaration order.

Multiple CHECK blocks are scheduled to execute in REVERSE declaration order.

Multiple INIT blocks are scheduled to execute in NORMAL declaration order.

Multiple END blocks are scheduled to execute in REVERSE declaration order.

An example containing several CHECK, INIT, normal code, and END blocks. The output shows the execution order:

```
END { print "END 1\n" }
CHECK { print "CHECK 1\n" }
BEGIN { print "BEGIN 1\n" }
INIT { print "INIT 1\n" }
print "normal\n";
INIT { print "INIT 2\n" }
BEGIN { print "BEGIN 2\n" }
CHECK { print "CHECK 2\n" }
END { print "END 2\n" }
> BEGIN 1
> BEGIN 2
> CHECK 2
> CHECK 1
> INIT 1
> INIT 2
> normal
> END 2
> END 1
```

12 Code Reuse, Perl Modules

Lets say you come up with some really great chunks of perl code that you want to use in several different programs. Perhaps you have some subroutines that are especially handy, and perhaps they have some private data associated with them. The best place to put code to be used in many different programs is in a "Perl Module", and then "use" that module. A perl module is really just a file with an invented name and a ".pm" extension. The "pm" is short for "perl module". If you had some handy code for modeling a dog, you might put it in a module called Dog.pm, and then you would use the "use" statement to read in the module.

The content of a perl module is any valid perl code. Generally, perl modules contain declarations, such as subroutine declarations and possibly declarations of private or public variables. These declared subroutines can be called and public variables can be accessed by any perl script that uses the module.

It is standard convention that all perl modules start out with a "package" declaration that declares the package namespace to be the same as the module name. After any new package declaration you will need to turn on warnings, etc.

Here is an example of our Dog module.

```
###filename: Dog.pm
package Dog;
use warnings; use strict; use Data::Dumper;
sub Speak { print "Woof!\n"; }
1; # MUST BE LAST STATEMENT IN FILE
```

All perl modules must end with "1;" otherwise you will get a compile error:
Dog.pm did not return a true value ...

13 The use Statement

The "use" statement allows a perl script to bring in a perl module and use whatever declarations have been made available by the module. Continuing our example, a file called script.pl could bring in the Dog module like this:

```
use Dog;
Dog::Speak;
> Woof!
```

Both files, Dog.pm and script.pl, would have to be in the same directory.

The Dog module declares its package namespace to be Dog. The module then declares a subroutine called "Speak", which, like any normal subroutine, ends up in the current package namespace, Dog. Once the Dog module has been used, anyone can call the subroutine by calling Dog::Speak;

14 The use Statement, Formally

The "use" statement can be formally defined as this:

```
use MODULENAME ( LISTOFARGS );
```

The "use" statement is exactly equivalent to this:

```
BEGIN
{
   require MODULENAME;
   MODULENAME->import( LISTOFARGS );
}
```

The MODULENAME follows the package namespace convention, meaning it would be either a single identifier or multiple identifiers separated by double-colons. These are all valid MODULENAMES:

```
use Dog;
use Pets::Dog;
use Pets::Dog::GermanShepard;
use Pets::Cat::Persian;
```

User created module names should be mixed case. Module names with all lower case are reserved for built in pragmas, such as "use warnings;" Module names with all upper case letters are just ugly and could get confused with built in words.

The "require" statement is what actually reads in the module file.

When performing the search for the module file, "require" will translate the double colons into whatever directory separator is used on your system. For Linux style systems, it would be a "/". So perl would look for Pets::Dog::GermanShepard in Pets/Dog/ for a file called GermanShepard.pm

14.1 The @INC Array

The "require" statement will look for the module path/file in all the directories listed in a global array called @INC. Perl will initialize this array to some default directories to look for any modules. If you want to create a subdirectory just for your modules, you can add this subdirectory to @INC and perl will find any modules located there.

Because the "require" statement is in a BEGIN block, though, it will execute immediately after being compiled. So this will not work:

```
push(@INC,'/home/username/perlmodules');
use Dogs;
```

This is because the "push" statement will get compiled and then be scheduled for execution after the entire program has been compiled. The "use" statement will get compiled and executed immediately (because it is exactly like a chunk of code in a BEGIN{} block. So the use Dogs will get executed BEFORE the path gets pushed into @INC.

You could say something like this:

```
BEGIN { push(@INC,'/home/username/perlmodules'); }
use Dogs;
```

An even better way to fix it is by invoking use lib

14.2 The use lib Statement

The "use lib" statement is my preferred way of adding directory paths to the @INC array, because it does not need a BEGIN block. Just say something like this:

```
use lib '/home/username/perlmodules';
```

Also, for you Linux heads, note that the home directory symbol "~" is only meaningful in a linux shell. Perl does not understand it. So if you want to include a directory under your home directory, you will need to call "glob" to translate "~" to something perl will understand. The "glob" function uses the shell translations on a path.

```
use lib glob('~/perlmodules');
use Dogs;
```

14.3 The PERL5LIB and PERLLIB Environment Variables

The "require" statement also searches for MODULENAME in any directories listed in the environment variable called PERL5LIB. The PERL5LIB variable is a colon separated list of directory paths. Consult your shell documentation to determine how to set this environment variable.

If you don't have PERL5LIB set, perl will search for MODULENAME in any directory listed in the PERLLIB environment variable.

14.4 The require Statement

Once the require statement has found the module, perl compiles it. Because the require statement is in a BEGIN block, the module gets executed immediately as well. This means any executable code gets executed. Any code that is not a declaration will execute at this point.

14.5 MODULENAME -> import (LISTOFARGS)

The MODULENAME->import(LISTOFARGS) statement is a "method call", which has not been introduced yet. A method call is a fancy way of doing a subroutine call with a couple of extra bells and whistles bolted on.

Basically, if your perl module declares a subroutine called "import" then it will get executed at this time.

More advancedly, one of the bells and whistles of a method call is a thing called "inheritance", which has not been introduced yet. So, to be more accurate, if your perl module OR ITS BASE CLASS(ES) declares a subroutine called "import" then it will get executed at this time.

The import method is a way for a module to import subroutines or variables to the caller's package. This happens when you use Data::Dumper in your script. Which is why you can say

```
use Data::Dumper;
print Dumper \@var;
```

instead of having to say:

```
use Data::Dumper;
print Data::Dumper::Dumper \@var;
```

A subroutine called "Dumper" from the package Data::Dumper gets imported into your package namespace.

14.6 The use Execution Timeline

The following example shows the complete execution timeline during a use statement.

```
#!/usr/local/env perl
###filename:script.pl
use warnings; use strict; use Data::Dumper;
warn "just before use Dog";
use Dog ('GermanShepard');
warn "just after use Dog";
Dog::Speak;
###filename:Dog.pm
package Dog;
use warnings; use strict; use Data::Dumper;
warn "executing normal code";
sub Speak { print "Woof!\n"; }
sub import {
   warn "calling import";
   print "with the following args\n";
   print Dumper \@_;
}
1; #MUST BE LAST STATEMENT IN FILE
> executing normal code at Dog.pm line 4.
> calling import at Dog.pm line 7.
> with the following args
> $VAR1 = [
>    'Dog',
>    'GermanShepard'
> ];
> just before use Dog at ./script.pl line 4.
> just after use Dog at ./script.pl line 6.
> Woof!
```

15 bless()

The bless() function is so simple that people usually have a hard time understanding it because they make it far more complicated than it really is. All bless does is change the string that would be returned when ref() is called. The bless() function is the basis for Object Oriented Perl, but bless() by itself is overwhelmingly simple.

Quick reference refresher: Given an array referent, @arr, and a reference, $rarr=\@arr, then calling ref($rarr) will return the string "ARRAY".

```
my @arr=(1,2,3); # referent
my $rarr = \@arr; # reference to referent
my $str = ref($rarr); # call ref()
warn "str is '$str'";
> str is 'ARRAY'
```

Normally, ref() will return SCALAR, ARRAY, HASH, CODE, or empty-string depending on what type of referent it is referred to.

```
warn ref(\4);
warn ref([]);
warn ref({});
warn ref(sub{});
warn "'".ref(4)."'";
> SCALAR at ./script.pl line 4.
> ARRAY at ./script.pl line 5.
> HASH at ./script.pl line 6.
> CODE at ./script.pl line 7.
> '' at ./script.pl line 8.
```

The bless function takes a reference and a string as input.

The bless function modifies the referent pointed to by the reference and attaches the given string such that ref() will return that string.

The bless function will then return the original reference.

```
bless REFERENCE, STRING;
```

Here is an example of bless() in action. Note this is exactly the same as the code in the first example, but with one line added to do the bless:

```
my @arr=(1,2,3); # referent
my $rarr = \@arr; # reference to referent
bless($rarr, "Counter");
my $str = ref($rarr); # call ref()
warn "str is '$str'";
> str is 'Counter'
```

Since bless() returns the reference, we can call ref() on the return value and accomplish it in one line:

```
my $sca=4;
warn ref(bless(\$sca,"Four"));
warn ref(bless([],"Box"));
warn ref(bless({},"Curlies"));
warn ref(bless(sub{},"Action"));
> Four at ./script.pl line 5.
> Box at ./script.pl line 6.
> Curlies at ./script.pl line 7.
> Action at ./script.pl line 8.
```

All bless() does is affect the value returned by ref(). That is it.

You might be wondering why the word "bless" was chosen. If a religious figure took water and blessed it, then people would refer to it as "holy water". The constitution and makeup of the water did not change, however it was given a new name, and because of that name it might be used differently.

In perl, bless() changes the name of a referent. It does not affect the contents of the referent, only the name returned by ref(). But because of this new name, the referent might be used differently or behave differently. We will see this difference with method calls.

16 Method Calls

We have seen method calls before. The MODULENAME->import(LISTOFARGS) was a method call, but we had to do some handwaving to get beyond it, calling it a fancy subroutine call.

Quick review of package qualified subroutine names: When you declare a subroutine, it goes into the current package namespace. You can call the subroutine using its short name if you are still in the package. Or you can use the fully qualified package name, and be guaranteed it will work every time.

```
package Dog;
sub Speak { print "Woof\n"; }
Speak;
Dog::Speak;
> Woof
> Woof
```

A method call is similar. Here is the generic definition:

```
INVOCANT -> METHOD ( LISTOFARGS );
```

The INVOCANT is the thing that "invoked" the METHOD. An invocant can be several different things, but the simplest thing it can be is just a bareword package name to go look for the subroutine called METHOD.

```
Dog -> Speak;
> Woof
```

So it is almost the same as using a package qualified subroutine name Dog::Speak. So what is different?

First, the INVOCANT always gets unshifted into the @_ array in the subroutine call.

```
package Dog;
use warnings; use strict; use Data::Dumper;
sub Speak {
    print Dumper \@_;
}
Dog -> Speak (3);
> $VAR1 = [
>    'Dog', # INVOCANT
>    3 # first user argument
> ];
```

This may not seem very useful, but an INVOCANT can be many different things, some more useful than others. The second difference between a subroutine call and a method call is inheritance.

16.1 Inheritance

Say you want to model several specific breeds of dogs. The specific breeds of dogs will likely be able to inherit some behaviors (subroutine/methods) from a base class that describes all dogs. Say we model a German Shepard that has the ability to track a scent better than other breeds. But German Shepards still bark like all dogs.

```
###filename:Dog.pm
package Dog;
use warnings; use strict; use Data::Dumper;
sub Speak {
   my ($invocant, $count) = @_;
   warn "invocant is '$invocant'";
   for(1 .. $count) { warn "Woof"; }
}
1;

###filename:Shepard.pm
package Shepard;
use base Dog;
sub Track { warn "sniff, sniff"; }
1;

#!/usr/local/env perl
###filename:script.pl
use Shepard;
Shepard->Speak(2);
Shepard->Track;
> invocant is 'Shepard' at Dog.pm line 6.
> Woof at Dog.pm line 8.
> Woof at Dog.pm line 8.
> sniff, sniff at Shepard.pm line 4.
```

Notice that script.pl used Shepard, not Dog. And script.pl always used Shepard as the invocant for its method calls. When script.pl called Shepard->Speak, perl first looked in the Shepard namespace for a subroutine called Shepard::Speak. It did not find one. So then it looked and found a BASE of Shepard called Dog. It then looked for a subroutine called Dog::Speak, found one, and called that subroutine.

Also notice that the subroutine Dog::Speak received an invocant of "Shepard". Even though perl ended up calling Dog::Speak, perl still passes Dog::Speak the original invocant, which was "Shepard" in this case.

Shepard INHERITED the Speak subroutine from the Dog package. The unexplained bit of magic is that inheritance uses the "use base" statement to determine what packages to inherit from.

16.2 *use base*

This statement:

```
use base MODULENAME;
```

is functionally identical to this:

```
BEGIN
{
    require MODULENAME;
    push(@ISA, MODULENAME);
}
```

The require statement goes and looks for MODULENAME.pm using the search pattern that we described in the "use" section earlier.

The push(@ISA,MODULENAME) is new. When a method call looks in a package namespace for a subroutine and does not find one, it will then go through the contents of the @ISA array. The @ISA array contains any packages that are BASE packages of the current package.

The @ISA array is named that way because "Shepard" IS A "Dog", therefore ISA. The search order is depth-first, left-to-right. This is not necessarily the "best" way to search, but it is how perl searches, so you will want to learn it. If this approach does not work for your application, you can change it with a module from CPAN.

Imagine a Child module has the following family inheritance tree:

```
Child.pm        => @ISA = qw ( Father Mother );
Father.pm       => @ISA = qw ( FathersFather FathersMother );
Mother.pm       => @ISA = qw ( MothersFather MothersMother );
FathersFather.pm => @ISA = ();
FathersMother.pm => @ISA = ();
MothersFather.pm => @ISA = ();
MothersMother.pm => @ISA = ();
```

Perl will search for Child->Method through the inheritance tree in the following order:

```
Child
Father
FathersFather
FathersMother
Mother
MothersFather
MothersMother
```

16.3 INVOCANT->isa(BASEPACKAGE)

The "isa" method will tell you if BASEPACKAGE exists anywhere in the @ISA inheritance tree.

```
Child->isa("MothersMother"); # TRUE
Child->isa("Shepard"); # FALSE
```

16.4 INVOCANT->can(METHODNAME)

The "can" method will tell you if the INVOCANT can call METHODNAME successfully.

```
Shepard->can("Speak"); # TRUE (努 oof
Child->can("Track"); # FALSE (can't track a scent)
```

16.5 Interesting Invocants

So far we have only used bareword invocants that correspond to package names.

```
Shepard->Track;
```

Perl allows a more interesting invocant to be used with method calls:

```
a blessed referent
```

Remember bless() changes the string returned by ref(). And also remember that when we make a method call, perl passes in the invocant as the first value in the @_ variable.

The difference here is that if the invocant is a REFERENCE, then perl doesn't pass the reference VARIABLE into @_. Instead, perl calls ref() on the invocant, and passes whatever string value ref(invocant) returns and passes THAT into @_.

Here is our simple Dog example but with a blessed invocant.

```
###filename:Dog.pm
package Dog;
use warnings; use strict; use Data::Dumper;
sub Speak {
   my ($invocant, $count) = @_;
   warn "invocant is '$invocant'";
   for(1 .. $count) { warn "Woof"; }
} 1;

#!/usr/local/env perl
###filename:script.pl
use Dog;
my $invocant=bless {},'Dog'; ### BLESSED INVOCANT
$invocant->Speak(2);

> invocant is 'Dog=HASH(0x8124394)' at Dog.pm line 6
> Woof at Dog.pm line 8.
> Woof at Dog.pm line 8.
```

The my $invocant=bless {},"Dog"; is the new line. The bless part creates an anonymous hash, {}, and blesses it with the name "Dog". If you called ref($invocant), it would return the string "Dog".

So perl uses $invocant, a hash blessed as a Dog as its invocant for the Speak method call. Perl takes $invocant and calls ref() on it, which returns the string Dog and so perl starts looking for a Speak() method in the Dog package.

17 Procedural Perl

So far, all the perl coding we have done has been "procedural" perl. When you hear "procedural" think of "Picard", as in Captain Picard of the starship Enterprise. Picard always gave the ship's computer commands in the form of procedural statements.

Computer, set warp drive to 5.
Computer, set shields to "off".
Computer, fire weapons: phasers and photon torpedoes.

The subject of the sentences was always "Computer". In procedural programming, the subject "computer" is implied, the way the subject "you" is implied in the sentence: "Stop!"

The verb and direct object of Picard's sentences become the subroutine name in proceedural programming. Whatever is left become arguments passed in to the subroutine call.

```
set_warp(5);
set_shield(0);
fire_weapons qw(phasers photon_torpedoes);
```

18 Object Oriented Perl

Object oriented perl does not use an implied "Computer" as the subject for its sentences. Instead, it uses what was the direct object in the procedural sentences and makes it the subject in object oriented programming.

```
Warp Drive, set yourself to 5.
Shields, set yourself to "off".
Phasors, fire yourself.
Torpedoes, fire yourself.
```

But how would we code these sentences?

Here is a minimal example of object oriented perl. There is a class called Animal. It has a constructor called MakeNew and a method called Speak. The script uses the Animal module, creates instances of Animal objects, and calls the Speak method on each one.

```perl
###filename:Animal.pm
package Animal;
sub MakeNew {                           # our constructor
    my ($invocant,$name)=@_;            # class and name passed in.
    my $object = {};                    # hash to store object data.
    $object->{Name}=$name;              # put name into hash.
    bless($object, $invocant);          # bless hash into class
    return $object;                     # return hash/instance/object
}

sub Speak {                             # some method
    my ($obj)=@_;                       # hash/instance/object passed in
    my $name = $obj->{Name};            # get name of this instance
    print "$name growls\n";             # say who is speaking
}
1;


#!/usr/local/env perl
###filename:script.pl
use Animal;

# note that 'Animal' is passed in to MakeNew
# as first parameter. 'Samson' is second parameter.
# 'Animal' becomes $invocant. 'Samson' becomes $name.
my $lion = Animal->MakeNew('Samson');  # create an instance

# note that the blessed hash reference, $lion, is passed
# into Speak method as first parameter. It becomes $obj.
$lion->Speak();   # call method on this instance

my $tiger = Animal->MakeNew('Fuzzball');
$tiger->Speak();

my $bear = Animal->MakeNew('Smokey');
$bear->Speak();

> Samson growls
> Fuzzball growls
> Smokey growls
```

So what? Basic Object Oriented does nothing that cannot be just as easily done in procedural perl. But once you start adding things like inheritance and polymorphism, the advantages of object oriented become more obvious.

The first thing we want to do is process objects as an array, rather than as individually named variables. Lets return to a familiar example, our Dog module.

```
###filename:Animal.pm
package Animal;
sub New {
    my ($invocant,$name)=@_;
    return bless({Name=>$name},$invocant);
} 1;

###filename:Dog.pm
package Dog;
use base Animal;
sub Speak {
    my ($obj)=@_;
    my $name=$obj->{Name};
    warn "$name says Woof";
} 1;

#!/usr/local/env perl
###filename:script.pl
use Dog;
my @pets;
# create 3 Dog objects and put them in @pets array
foreach my $name (qw(Butch Spike Fluffy)) {
    push(@pets, Dog->New($name));
}
# have every pet speak for themselves.
foreach my $pet (@pets) { $pet->Speak; }

> Butch says Woof at Dog.pm line 7.
> Spike says Woof at Dog.pm line 7.
> Fluffy says Woof at Dog.pm line 7.
```

Notice the last foreach loop in script.pl says $pet->Speak. This is object oriented programming, because if you translated that statement to English, it would be "Pet, speak for yourself". The subject of the sentence is "Pet", rather than the implied "Computer" of procedural programming.

Object Oriented Programming statements are of the form:
```
$subject -> verb ( adjectives, adverbs, etc );
```

18.1 Class

The term "class" refers to a perl package/module that is used in an object oriented way. A perl package that is designed for procedural use is simply called a package. If it's an OO package, you can call it a ClassPolymorphism

Polymorphism is a real fancy way of saying having different types of objects that have the same methods. Expanding our previous example, we might want to add a Cat class to handle cats at the pet store.

```
###filename:Cat.pm
package Cat;
use base Animal;
sub Speak {
   my $obj=shift;
   my $name=$obj->{Name};
   warn "$name says Meow";
} 1;
```

Then we modify script.pl to put some cats in the @pets array.

```
#!/usr/local/env perl
###filename:script.pl
use Dog; use Cat;
my @pets;
#create some dog objects
foreach my $name (qw(Butch Spike Fluffy)) {
    push(@pets, Dog->New($name));
}
# create some cat objects
foreach my $name (qw(Fang Furball Fluffy)) {
   push(@pets, Cat->New($name));
}
# have all the pets say something.
foreach my $pet (@pets) {
   $pet->Speak; # polymorphism at work
}

> Butch says Woof at Dog.pm line 7.
> Spike says Woof at Dog.pm line 7.
> Fluffy says Woof at Dog.pm line 7.
> Fang says Meow at Cat.pm line 7.
> Furball says Meow at Cat.pm line 7.
> Fluffy says Meow at Cat.pm line 7.
```

Notice how the last loop goes through all the pets and has each one speak for themselves. Whether its a dog or cat, the animal will say whatever is appropriate for its type. This is polymorphism. The code processes a bunch of objects and calls the same method on each object. And each object just knows how to do what it should do.

18.2 SUPER

SUPER:: is an interesting bit of magic that allows a child object with a method call that same method name in its parent's class.

Back to the dogs. To shorten the example, the constructor New was moved to Dog.pm. The Shepard module uses Dog as its base, and has a Speak method that growls, and then calls its ancestor's Dog version of speak.

```perl
###filename:Dog.pm
package Dog;
sub New {
   return bless({Name=>$_[1]},$_[0]);
}
sub Speak {
   my $name=$_[0]->{Name};
   warn "$name says Woof";
} 1;

###filename:Shepard.pm
package Shepard;
use base Dog;
sub Speak {
   my $name=$_[0]->{Name};
   warn "$name says Grrr";
   $_[0]->SUPER::Speak; ### name says woof
} 1;

#!/usr/local/env perl
###filename:script.pl
use warnings; use strict; use Data::Dumper;
use Shepard;
my $dog=Shepard->New("Spike");
$dog->Speak;

> Spike says Grrr at Shepard.pm line 6.
> Spike says Woof at Dog.pm line 8.
```

Without the magic of SUPER, the only way that Shepard can call Dog's version of speak is to use a fully package qualified name Dog::Speak(); But this scatters hardcoded names of the base class throughout Shepard, which would make changing the base class a lot of work.

If Shepard's version of Speak simply said $_[0]->Speak, it would get into an infinite loop calling itself recursively. SUPER is a way of saying, "look at my ancestors and call their version of this method."

There are some limitations with SUPER. Consider the big family tree inheritance in the "use base" section of this document (the one with Child as the root, Father and Mother as parents, and FathersFather, FathersMother, etc as grandparents).

Imagine an object of type "Child". If "Father" has a method called Speak and that method calls SUPER::Speak, the only modules that will get looked at is "FathersFather" and "FathersMother". SUPER looks up the hierarchy starting at the class from where it was called. This means if the method FathersFather needed to call was in MothersMother, then SUPER will not work.

This could be considered a good thing, since you would assume that Father was designed only knowing about FathersFather and FathersMother. When Father was coded, MothersMother was a complete stranger he would not meet for years to come. So designing Father to rely on his future, have-not-even-met-her-yet mother-in-law, could be considered a bad thing.

However, it is legitimate to have what you might consider to be "universal" methods that exist for every class. Instead of a class called "Child" imagine a class called "CoupleAboutToGetMarried", and every base class has a method called "ContributeToWedding". In that case, every class could do its part, and then call SUPER::ContributeToWedding. The FatherOfTheBride would pay for the wedding, the FatherOfTheGroom would pay for the rehersal dinner, and so on and so forth.

Unfortunately, there is no easy, built-in way to do this in perl.

I will refer you to the "NEXT.pm" module available on CPAN.

SUPER does have its uses, though. Many times a class might exist that does ALMOST what you want it to do. Rather than modify the original code to do what you want it to, you could instead create a derived class that inherits the base class and rewrite the method to do what you want it to do. For example, you might want a method that calls its parent method but then multiplies the result by minus one or something. In cases like this, SUPER will do the trick.

18.3 Object Destruction

Object destruction occurs when all the references to a specific object have gone out of lexical scope, and the object is scheduled for garbage collection. Just prior to deleting the object and any of its internal data, perl will call the DESTROY method on the object. If no such method exists, perl silently moves on and cleans up the object data.

```
###filename:Dog.pm
package Dog;
sub New {
   return bless({Name=>$_[1]},$_[0]);
}
sub DESTROY {
   warn (($_[0]->{Name})." has been sold");
} 1;

#!/usr/local/env perl
###filename:script.pl
use warnings; use strict; use Data::Dumper;
use Dog;
my $dog=Dog->New("Spike");
$dog=undef;

> Spike has been sold at Dog.pm line 7.
```

The DESTROY method has similar limitations as SUPER. With an object that has a complex hierarchical family tree, perl will only call the FIRST method of DESTROY that it finds in the ancestry. If Mother and Father both have a DESTROY method, then Mother's not going to handle her demise properly and you will likely have ghosts when you run your program.

The NEXT.pm module on CPAN also solves this limitation.

19 Object Oriented Review

19.1 Modules

The basis for code reuse in perl is a module. A perl module is a file that ends in ".pm" and declares a package namespace that (hopefully) matches the name of the file. The module can be designed for procedural programming or object oriented programming (OO). If the module is OO, then the module is sometimes referred to as a "class".

19.2 use Module

The code in a perl module can be made available to your script by saying "use MODULE;" The "use" statement will look for the module in the directories listed in the PERL5LIB environment variable and then the directories listed in the @INC variable.

The best way to add directories to the @INC variable is to say

```
use lib "/path/to/dir";
```

Any double-colons (::) in the module name being used get converted to a directory separator symbol of the operating system.

19.3 bless / constructors

Constructors are subroutines that create a reference to some variable, use the reference to bless the variable into the class, and then return the reference as an object. The object is usually a hash reference. Keys to the hash correspond to object attribute names, and the hash values correspond to the attribute values for that particular instance.

Constructors can be named anything, but it is suggested to use new. One easy way to design all your constructors is to require callers pass in all attribute/value pairs, such as (Name=>'Fluffy'). Your first draft constructor would look like this:

```perl
sub new {
   my $class=shift(@_);
   return bless( { @_ } , $class);
}


Your first draft of a constructor call would look like this:

my $dog = Dog->new(Name=>'Fluffy');
```

You can then modify your constructor code later to enforce required parameters, put default values to parameters not given, and so on. For example:

```perl
package MyClass;
use Carp;   #handy die messaging through croak sub.
my $new_object_attributes={ # define all valid attributes
    Name=>undef,
    Age=>0,        # default values
};
sub new {
   my $class=shift(@_);
   my %params=(@_);
   my $obj= bless({},$class);
   while(my($key,$val)=each(%params)){
        unless(exists($new_object_attributes->{$key}))
           {croak "Error: bad attribute '$key'"}
        $obj->{$key}=$val;
   }
   while(my($key,$val)=each(%$new_object_attributes)){
        warn "key is '$key'. Val is '$val'"
        unless(exists($obj->{$key}))
            {$obj->{$key}=$new_object_attributes->{$key};}
   }
   return $obj;
}
1;
```

19.4 Methods

Once an instance of an object has been constructed, methods can be called on the instance to get information, change values, perform operations, etc. A method is simply a subroutine that receives a reference to the instance variable as its first argument. Methods should be thought of as "actions" to be performed on the instance, or "verbs" in a sentences with instances being the "subject".

In the above examples, "Speak" was a method that used the Name of the instance to print out "$name says woof". The preferred way of calling a method is using the arrow method.

```
$ObjectInstance -> Method ( list of arguments );
```

In the Animal.pm example, this would look like:

```
$pet->Speak;
```

19.5 Inheritance

Classes can inherit methods from base classes. This allows many similar classes to put all their common methods in a single base class. To have a class inherit from a base class, use the "use base" statement.

```
use base BaseClassName;
```

In one example above, the Cat and Dog classes both inherit from a common Animal class. Both Dog and Cat classes inherit the constructor "New" method from the Animal base class.

The classes Cat and Dog inherit from the base class Animal. Cat and Dog are "derived" from Animal.

19.6 Overriding Methods and SUPER

Classes can override the methods of their base classes. If a base class contains a method called "MethodName", then a derived class can override the base class method by declaring its own subroutine called MethodName.

In the examples above, the GermanShepard derived class overrode the Dog base class Speak method with its own method.

If a derived class overrides a method of its base class, it may want to call its base class method. The only way to accomplish this is with the SUPER:: pseudopackage name. The GermanShepard method named Speak called the Dog version of Speak by calling:

```
$obj->SUPER::Speak;
```

19.7 Object Oriented and Moose.pm and Perl 6

The object oriented approach built into perl 5 is a bit problematic. Constructors can use any type of container reference they want. But if one class uses an array reference and another class uses a hash reference, then those classes can never inherit from one another. There is also no concept of private data in a class. All data is usually stored in the same hash ref for the object, and all data can be dereferenced if the key name is known.

As problematic as it CAN be, there are some good, useful modules out there that use perl 5's approach to OO. Therefore it is good to know and understand how perl 5 OO programming works. When you download a module from CPAN, there's a good chance it will use object oriented techniques. So you will want to understand how OO perl 5 works so you can effectively use those modules on CPAN.

Perl 6 is spec'ed out to fix a number of issues with OO perl 5. But Perl 6 is not yet available.

In the mean time, anyone creating NEW object oriented code in Perl 5 is recommended to look into a module on CPAN called Moose.pm.

20 CPAN

CPAN is an acronym for "Comprehensive Perl Archive Network". There is a CPAN website, which contains a plethora of perl module for anyone to download. There is also a CPAN perl module, which provides a shell interface for automating the downloading of perl modules from the CPAN website. A "perldoc" utility comes with perl that allows viewing of POD, which is "Plain Old Documentation" embedded within the perl modules downloaded from CPAN. And finally, there is a "h2xs" utility, which automates the creation of a module to be uploaded to CPAN.

20.1 CPAN, The Web Site

CPAN is a website that contains all things perl: help, FAQs, source code to install perl, and most importantly, a plethora of perl module so that you can re-use someone else's code.
http://www.cpan.org

CPAN contains a number of search engines. Once you find a module that might do what you need, you can view the README file that is usually available online before actually downloading the module. If the README looks promising, then download the tarball, which will be a file with a tar.gz extension. Here is the standard installation steps for a module. This example is for the NEXT.pm module, which is contained in NEXT-0.60.tar.gz (you should use the latest version, if available.)

```
> gunzip NEXT-0.60.tar.gz
> tar -xf NEXT-0.60.tar
> cd NEXT-0.60
```

From here, most modules install with the exact same commands:

```
> perl Makefile.PL
> make
> make test
> su root
> make install
> exit
```

The "make install" step requires root privileges. The "exit" step is shown just so you remember to log out from root.

If you do not have root privileges and the module is pure perl (just a .pm file), then you can copy the .pm file to your home directory (or anywhere you have read/write privileges), and then set your PERL5LIB environment variable to point to that directory.

20.2 cpanm, The Perl Module Installer

The cpanm ("cpan minus") script is an automatic perl module installer. You tell it what module to install, and it goes and gets it from CPAN and installs it. If the module has dependencies, cpanm automatically installs them too. It's a lot easier than the manual approach.

To install cpanm, try the following:

```
> # log in as root however you do that
> sudo su root
>
> # install cpanm
> cpan App::cpanminus
```

If it asks if you want to configure things manually, try "no". It should then auto configure itself, and then it will try to install itself and a bunch of dependencies. Every time it asks you if you want to add dependencies to the queue of modules to install, say "yes".

Whenever you want to run cpanm, log in as root, then run the cpanm command. To see if it was installed properly, log in as root and try this:

```
> cpanm --self-upgrade
```

20.3 Creating Modules for CPAN with Module::Starter

If you wish to create a module that you intend to upload to CPAN, download the Module::Starter module using cpanm. Once it is installed, you can create a skeleton of the module you want with the command:

```
module-starter --module=Foo::Bar,Foo::Bat \
        --author="Andy Lester" --email=andy@petdance.com
```

Edit the module to have the behavior you want, then create a tarball for uploading to CPAN with the following commands:

```
> perl Makefile.PL
> make
> make test
> su root
> make dist
```

This will create a tarball with a name like Foo-Bar-(revisionnumber).tar.gz. You can then upload this to CPAN and then other people can automatically install it with cpanm.

21 The Next Level

You now know the fundamentals of procedural perl and object oriented perl. From this point forward, any new topics may include a discussion of a perl builtin feature or something available from CPAN. Some of perl's builtin features are somewhat limited and a CPAN module greatly enhances and/or simplifies its usage.

22 Command Line Arguments

Scripts are often controlled by the arguments passed into it via the command line when the script is executed. Arguments might be a switch, such as "-h" to get help.

```
> myscript.pl -h
```

A "-v" switch might turn verboseness on.

```
> anotherscript.pl -v
```

Switches might be followed by an argument associated with the switch. A "-in" switch might be followed by a filename to be used as input.

```
> thatscript.pl -in data.txt
```

An argument could indicate to stop processing the remaining arguments and to process them at a later point in the script. The "--" argument could be used to indicate that arguments before it are to be used as perl arguments and that arguments after it are to be passed directly to a compiler program that the script will call.

```
> mytest.pl -in test42.txt -- +define+FAST
```

More advanced arguments:

Single character switches can be lumped together. Instead of "-x -y -z", you could say "-xyz".

Options can be stored in a separate file. A file might contain a number of options always needed to do a standard function, and using "-f optionfile.txt" would be easier than putting those options on the command line each and every time that function is needed. This would allow a user to use the option file and then add other options on the command line.

```
> thisscript.pl -f optionfile.txt -v
```

Options can have full and abbreviated versions to activate the same option.

The option "-verbose" can also work as "-v". Options operate independent of spacing.

```
-f=options.txt
-f = options.txt
```

22.1 @ARGV

Perl provides access to all the command line arguments via a global array @ARGV. The text on the command line is broken up anywhere whitespace occurs, except for quoted strings.

```
#!/usr/bin/env perl
###filename:script.pl
use warnings; use strict; use Data::Dumper;
print Dumper \@ARGV;

> script.pl -v -f options.txt "hello world"
> $VAR1 = [
>     '-v',
>     '-f',
>     'options.txt',
>     'hello world'
> ];
```

If you need to pass in a wild-card such as *.txt then you will need to put it in quotes or your operating system will replace it with a list of files that match the wildcard pattern.

```
#!/usr/bin/env perl
###filename:script.pl
use warnings; use strict; use Data::Dumper;
print Dumper \@ARGV;

> ./test.pl *.pl
> $VAR1 = [
>     'script.pl',
>     'test.pl'
> ];
> ./test.pl "*.pl"
> $VAR1 = [
>     '*.pl'
> ];
```

An example of simple +arg and +arg=value command line argument handling might look like this:

```perl
my $arguments;
my $default_argument_values={ #put all valid arguments here
    '-h'=>0,                         # default values too
    '-name'=>"Bob",
    '+verbose'=>0,
};

while(scalar(@ARGV)){
   my $next=shift(@ARGV);
   my ($arg,$val)=split(/\=/, $next, 2);
   unless($next=~m{\=}){$val=1;}
   unless(exists($default_argument_values->{$arg}))
       {die "ERROR: invalid command line arg '$arg'";}
   if(exists($arguments->{$arg}))
       {die "ERROR: duplicate command line arg '$arg'";}
   $arguments->{$arg}=$val;
}
while(my($key,$val)=each(%$default_argument_values)){
   unless(exists($arguments->{$key}))
       {$arguments->{$key}=$default_argument_values->{$key};}
}

print Dumper $arguments;
# now use $arguments hash to get the value of an argument.
```

The advantage of the above code is that you only have to define the default_argument_values hash with all the supported arguments and their default values. The rest of the code remains the same. At the end of the code block, the hash reference, $arguments, contains all the command line arguments as well as any arguments not provided by the command line, with their default values assigned.

If the user enters an invalid argument, or the same argument more than once, it dies.

22.2 Getopt::Declare

The Getopt::Declare module allows for an easy way to define more complicated command line arguments. An example of handling -h,-f, and -d options could be written using Getopt::Declare like this:

```perl
use Getopt::Declare;
our $fn='';
our $debug=0;
my $args = Getopt::Declare->new( q (
   -in <filename> Define input file
       {$main::fn=$filename;}
   -d Turn debugging On
       {$main::debug=1;}
   <unknown>
       { die "unknown arg '$unknown'\n"; }
));
print "Debug is '$debug'\n";
print "fn is '$fn'\n";
```

The text passed into Getopt::Declare is a multi-line quoted q() string. This string defines the arguments that are acceptable. Notice that -h is not defined in the string. This is because Getopt::Declare recognizes -h to print out help based on the declaration.

```
> script.pl -h
>Options:
> -in <filename> Define input file
> -d Turn debugging On
```

The argument declaration and the argument description is separated by one or more tabs in the string passed into Getopt::Declare.

The <unknown> marker is used to define what action to take with unknown arguments, arguments that are not defined in the declaration.

The text within the curly braces {$main::fn=$filename;} is treated as executable code and evaled if the declared argument is encountered on the command line. Note that within the curly braces, the global variables $fn and $debug are used with their full package name. Also, not that the starting curly brace must begin on its own line separate from the argument declaration and description.

Getopt::Declare recognizes -v as a version command line argument. If -v is on the command line, it will print out the version of the file based on $main::VERSION (if it exists) and the date the file was saved.

If [undocumented] is contained anywhere in the command line argument description, then that argument will not be listed in the help text, but will still be recognized if placed on the command line (secret arguments)

A [ditto] flag in the description will use the same text description as the argument just before it, and any action associated with it.

A short and long version of the same argument can be listed by placing the optional second half in square brackets: -verb[ose] This will recognize -verb and -verbose as the same argument.

Normally, a declared argument will only be allowed to occur on the command line once. If the argument can occur more than once, place [repeatable] in the description. Inside the curly braces, calling finish() with a true value will cause the command line arguments to stop being processed at that point.

22.2.1 Getopt::Declare Sophisticated Example

The example on the next page shows Getopt::Declare being used more to its potential.

1. Filenames to be handled by the script can be listed on the command line without any argument prefix
2. Verbosity can be turned on with -verbose. It can be turned off with -quiet.
3. An undocumented -Dump option turns on dumping.
4. Any options after a double dash (--) are left in @ARGV for later processing.
5. Additional arguments can be placed in an external file and loaded with -args filename.

The Error() subroutine will report the name of the file containing any error while processing the arguments. Argument files can refer to other argument files, allowing nested argument files.

6. Any arguments that are not defined will generate an error.

```perl
# advanced command line argument processing
use Getopt::Declare;
our $arg_file='Command Line';
our $VERSION=1.01; # -v will use this
our @files;
our $debug=0;
our $verbose=0;
our $dump=0;
sub Verbose {if($verbose){print $_[0];}}
sub Error {die"Error: ".($_[0])." from '$arg_file'\n";}
my $grammar = q(
    -args <input> Arg file [repeatable]
        { unless(-e $input)
            {main::Error("no file '$input'");}
          main::Verbose("Parsing '$input'\n");
          { local($main::arg_file);
            $main::arg_file = $input;
            $main::myparser->parse([$input]);
          }
          main::Verbose ("finished parsing '$input'\n");
          main::Verbose ("returning to '$main::arg_file'\n");
        }
    -d    Turn debugging On
            {$main::debug=1;}
    -verb[ose] Turn verbose On
       {$main::verbose=1;}
    -quiet Turn verbose Off
       {$main::verbose=0;}
    --Dump [undocumented] Dump on
       {$main::dump=1;}
    -h Print Help
       {$main::myparser->usage;}
    -- Argument separator
       {finish(1);}
    <unknown> Filename [repeatable]
        { if($unknown!~m{^[-+]})
            {push(@main::files,$unknown);}
          else
            {main::Error("unknown arg '$unknown'");}
        }
);

our $myparser = new Getopt::Declare
($grammar,['-BUILD']);
$myparser->parse();
```

23 File Input and Output

Perl has a number of functions used for reading from and writing to files. All file IO revolves around file handles.

To generate a filehandle and attach it to a specific file, use the open() function.

```
open(my $filehandle, 'filename.txt')
    or die "Could not open file";
```

If the first argument to open() is an undefined scalar, perl will create a filehandle and assign it to that scalar. This is available in perl version 5.6 and later and is the preferred method for dealing with filehandles.

The second argument to open() is the name of the file and an optional flag that indicates to open the file as read, write, or append. The filename is a simple string, and the flag, if present, is the first character of the string. The valid flags are defined as follows:

```
'<' Read. Do not create.
    Do not clobber existing file. DEFAULT.
'>' Write. Create if non-existing.
    Clobber if already exists.
'>>' Append. Create if non-existing.
    Do not clobber existing file.
```

If no flag is specified, the file defaults to being opened for read.

23.1 close

Once open, you can close a filehandle by calling the close function and passing it the filehandle.

```
close($filehandle) or die "Could not close";
```

If the filehandle is stored in a scalar, and the scalar goes out of scope or is assigned undef, then perl will automatically close the filehandle for you.

23.2 read

Once open, you can read from a filehandle a number of ways. The most common is to read the filehandle a line at a time using the "angle" operator. The angle operator is the filehandle surrounded by angle brackets. i.e. <$filehandle> When used as the boolean conditional controlling a while() loop, the loop reads the filehandle a line at a time until the end of file is reached. Each pass reads the next line from the file and places it in the $_ variable.

This script shows a cat -n style function.
```perl
open (my $fh, 'input.txt') or die "could not open";
my $num=0;
while(<$fh>) {
    $num++;
    my $line = $_;
    chomp($line);
    print "$num: $line\n";
}
```

The above example is useful if every line of the file contains the same kind of information, and you are just going through each line and parsing it.

Another way to read from a filehandle is to assign the angle operator of the filehandle to a scalar. This will read the next line from the filehandle. But it requires that you test the return value to make sure it is defined, otherwise you hit the end of file.

```perl
defined(my $line = <$fh>) or die "premature eof";
```

To make a little more useful, you can wrap it up in a subroutine to hide the error checking. You can then call the subroutine each time you want a line. This is useful if you are reading a file where every line has a different meaning, and you need to read it in a certain order.

```perl
use Carp;
open (my $fh, 'input.txt');
sub nlin {
    defined(my $line =<$fh>) or croak "premature eof";
    chomp($line);
    return $line;
}
my $name=nlin;
my $addr=nlin;
my $age =nlin;
print "Name: $name, address: $addr, age: $age\n";
```

23.3 write

If the file is opened for write or append, you can write to the filehandle using the print function.

```
open (my $fh, '>output.txt');
print $fh "once\n";
print $fh "upon\n";
print $fh "a time\n";
close $fh;
```

23.4 File Tests

Perl can perform tests on a file to glean information about the file. All tests return a true (1) or false ("") value about the file. All the tests have the following syntax:

```
-x FILE
```

The "x" is a single character indicating the test to perform. FILE is a filename (string) or filehandle.

Some common tests include:

```
-e file exists
-f file is a plain file
-d file is a directory
-l file is a symbolic link
-r file is readable
-w file is writable
-z file size is zero
-p file is a named pipe
-S file is a socket
-T file is a text file (perl's definition)
```

23.5 File Globbing

The glob() function takes a string expression and returns a list of files that match that expression using shell style filename expansion and translation.

```
my @files = glob ( STRING_EXPRESSION );
```

For example, if you wish to get a list of all the files that end with a .txt expression:

```
my @textfiles = glob ("*.txt");
```

This is also useful to translate Linux style "~" home directories to a usable file path.

```
my $startup_file = glob('~/.cshrc');
```

23.6 File Tree Searching

For sophisticated searching, including searches down an entire directory structure, use the File::Find module. It is included in perl 5.6.1.

```
use File::Find;
my $pwd=`pwd`;
chomp($pwd);
find(\&process,$pwd);
sub process { ... }
```

The process() subroutine is a subroutine that you define. The process() subroutine will be called on every file and directory in $pwd and recursively into every subdirectory and file below.

The package variable $File::Find::name contains the name of the current file or directory. Your process() subroutine can read this variable and perform whatever testing it wants on the fullname. If you process() was called on a file and not just a directory, the path to the file is available in $File::Find::dir and the name of the file is in $_. If your process() subroutine sets the package variable $File::Find::prune to 1, then find() will not recurse any further into the current directory.

This process() subroutine prints out all .txt files encountered and it avoids entering any CVS directories.

```
sub process {
    my $fullname = $File::Find::name;
    if ($fullname =~ m{\.txt$})
        {print "found text file $fullname\n";}
    if((-d $fullname) and ($fullname=~m{CVS}))
        {$File::Find::prune=1; return;}
}
```

For more information: perldoc File::Find

24 Operating System Commands

Two ways to issue operating system commands within your perl script are the system function and the backtick operator.

```
1.system("command string");
2.`command string`;
```

A third way to issue an operating system command within a perl script is with the pipe command. The pipe command is currently not covered in Impatient Perl.

24.1 The system() function

If you want to execute some command and you do not care what the output looks like, you just want to know if it worked, then you will likely want to use the system() function. The system() function executes the command string in a shell and returns you the return code of the command. In Linux, a return value of ZERO is usually good, a non-zero indicates some sort of error. So to use the system() function and check the return value, you might do something like this:

```
my $cmd = "rm -f junk.txt";
system($cmd)==0 or die "Error: could not '$cmd'";
```

When you execute a command via the system() function, the output of the command goes to STDOUT, which means the user will see the output scroll by on the screen, and then it is lost forever.

24.2 The Backtick Operator

If you want to capture the STDOUT of a operating system command, then you will want to use the backtick operator. A simple example is the "finger" command on Linux. If you type:

```
linux> finger username
```

Linux will dump a bunch of text to STDOUT. If you call system() on the finger command, all this text will go to STDOUT and will be seen by the user when they execute your script. If you want to capture what goes to STDOUT and manipulate it within your script, use the backtick operator.

```
my $string_results = `finger username`;
```

The $string_results variable will contain all the text that would have gone to STDOUT. You can then process this in your perl script like any other string.

24.3 Operating System Commands in a GUI

If your perl script is generating a GUI using the Tk package, there is a third way to run system commands within your perl script, using the Tk::ExecuteCommand module. This is a very cool module that allows you to run system commands in the background as a separate process from your main perl script. The module provides the user with a "Go/Cancel" button and allows the user to cancel the command in the middle of execution if it is taking too long.

We have not covered the GUI toolkit for perl (Tk), but if you are doing system commands in perl and you are using Tk, you should look into Tk::ExecuteCommand.

25 Regular Expressions

Regular expressions are the text processing workhorse of perl. With regular expressions, you can search strings for patterns, find out what matched the patterns, and substitute the matched patterns with new strings.

There are three different regular expression operators in perl:
```
1.match       m{PATTERN}
2.substitute  s{OLDPATTERN}{NEWPATTERN}
3.transliterate tr{OLD_CHAR_SET}{NEW_CHAR_SET}
```

Perl allows any delimiter in these operators, such as {} or () or // or ## or just about any character you wish to use. The most common delimiter used is probably the m// and s/// delimiters, but I prefer to use m{} and s{}{} because they are clearer for me. There are two ways to "bind" these operators to a string expression:

```
1.=~ pattern does match string expression
2.!~ pattern does NOT match string expression
```

Binding can be thought of as "Object Oriented Programming" for regular expressions. Generic OOP structure can be represented as

```
$subject -> verb ( adjectives, adverbs, etc );
```

Binding in Regular Expressions can be looked at in a similar fashion:

```
$string =~ verb ( pattern );
```

where "verb" is limited to 'm' for match, 's' for substitution, and 'tr' for translate. You may see perl code that simply looks like this:

```
/patt/;
```

This is functionally equivalent to this:

```
$_ =~ m/patt/;
```

Here are some examples:

```
# spam filter
my $email = "This is a great Free Offer\n";
if($email =~ m{Free Offer})
   {$email="*deleted spam*\n"; }
print "$email\n";

# upgrade my car
my $car = "my car is a toyota\n";
$car =~ s{toyota}{jaguar};
print "$car\n";

# simple encryption, Caesar cypher
my $love_letter = "How I love thee.\n";
$love_letter =~ tr{A-Za-z}{N-ZA-Mn-za-m};
print "encrypted: $love_letter";

$love_letter =~ tr{A-Za-z}{N-ZA-Mn-za-m};
print "decrypted: $love_letter\n";

> *deleted spam*
> my car is a jaguar
> encrypted: Ubj V ybir gurr.
> decrypted: How I love thee.
```

The above examples all look for fixed patterns within the string. Regular expressions also allow you to look for patterns with different types of "wildcards".

25.1 Variable Interpolation

The braces that surround the pattern act as double-quote marks, subjecting the pattern to one pass of variable interpolation as if the pattern were contained in double-quotes. This allows the pattern to be contained within variables and interpolated during the regular expression.

```
my $actual = "Toyota";
my $wanted = "Jaguar";
my $car = "My car is a Toyota\n";
$car =~ s{$actual}{$wanted};
print $car;

> My car is a Jaguar
```

25.2 Wildcard Example

In the example below, we process an array of lines, each containing the pattern {filename: } followed by one or more non-whitespace characters forming the actual filename. Each line also contains the pattern {size: } followed by one or more digits that indicate the actual size of that file.

```
my @lines = split "\n", <<"MARKER"
filename: output.txt size: 1024
filename: input.dat size: 512
filename: address.db size: 1048576
MARKER
;
foreach my $line (@lines) {
   #####################################
   # \S is a wildcard meaning
   # "anything that is not white-space".
   # the "+" means "one or more"
   #####################################
   if($line =~ m{filename: (\S+)}) {
      my $name = $1;
      ###########################
      # \d is a wildcard meaning
      # "any digit, 0-9".
      ###########################
      $line =~ m{size: (\d+)};
      my $size = $1;
      print "$name,$size\n";
   }
}
> output.txt,1024
> input.dat,512
> address.db,1048576
```

25.3 Defining a Pattern

A pattern can be a literal pattern such as {Free Offer}. It can contain wildcards such as {\d}. It can also contain metacharacters such as the parenthesis. Notice in the above example, the parenthesis were in the pattern but did not occur in the string, yet the pattern matched.

25.4 Metacharacters

Metacharacters do not get interpreted as literal characters. Instead they tell perl to interpret the metacharacter (and sometimes the characters around metacharacter) in a different way. The following are metacharacters in perl regular expression patterns:

      \ | ( ) [ ] { } ^ $ * + ? .

\\   (backslash) if next character combined with this backslash forms a character class shortcut, then match that character class. If not a shortcut, then simply treat next character as a non-metacharacter.

| alternation: (patt1 | patt2) means (patt1 OR patt2)
()   grouping (clustering) and capturing
(?:) grouping (clustering), no capturing. (somewhat faster)
.   match any single character (usually not "\n")
[]   define character class, match any single character in class
*   (quantifier): match previous item zero or more times
+   (quantifier): match previous item one or more times
?   (quantifier): match previous item zero or one time
{}   (quantifier): match previous item a number of times in given range
^   (position marker): beginning of string (or possibly after "\n")
$ (position marker): end of string (or possibly before "\n")

Examples below. Change the value assigned to $str and re-run the script. Experiment with what matches and what does not match the different regular expression patterns.

```perl
my $str = "Dear sir, hello and goodday! "
." dogs and cats and sssnakes put me to sleep."
." zzzz. Hummingbirds are ffffast. "
." Sincerely, John";
# | alternation
# match "hello" or "goodbye"
if($str =~ m{hello|goodbye}){warn "alt";}

# () grouping and capturing
# match 'goodday' or 'goodbye'
if($str =~ m{(good(day|bye))})
    {warn "group matched, captured '$1'";}

# . any single character
# match 'cat' 'cbt' 'cct' 'c%t' 'c+t' 'c?t' ...
if($str =~ m{c.t}){warn "period";}

# [] define a character class: 'a' or 'o' or 'u'
# match 'cat' 'cot' 'cut'
if($str =~ m{c[aou]t}){warn "class";}

# * quantifier, match previous item zero or more
# match '' or 'z' or 'zz' or 'zzz' or 'zzzzzzz'
if($str =~ m{z*}){warn "asterisk";}

# + quantifier, match previous item one or more
# match 'snake' 'ssnake' 'sssssssnake'
if($str =~ m{s+nake}){warn "plus sign";}

# ? quantifier, previous item is optional
# match only 'dog' and 'dogs'
if($str =~ m{dogs?}){warn "question";}

# {} quantifier, match previous, 3 <= qty <= 5
# match only 'fffast', 'ffffast', and 'fffffast'
if($str =~ m{f{3,5}ast}){warn "curly brace";}

# ^ position marker, matches beginning of string
# match 'Dear' only if it occurs at start of string
if($str =~ m{^Dear}){warn "caret";}

# $ position marker, matches end of string
# match 'John' only if it occurs at end of string
if($str =~ m{John$}){warn "dollar";}
> alt at ...
> group matched, captured 'goodday' at ...
> period at ...
> class at ...
> asterisk at ...
> plus sign at ...
> question at ...
> curly brace at ...
> caret at ...
> dollar at ...
```

25.5 Capturing and Clustering Parenthesis

Normal parentheses will both cluster and capture the pattern they contain. Clustering affects the order of evaluation similar to the way parentheses affect the order of evaluation within a mathematical expression. Normally, multiplication has a higher precedence than addition. The expression "2 + 3 * 4" does the multiplication first and then the addition, yielding the result of "14". The expression "(2 + 3) * 4" forces the addition to occur first, yielding the result of "20".

Clustering parentheses work in the same fashion. The pattern {cats?} will apply the "?" quantifier to the letter "s", matching either "cat" or "cats". The pattern {(cats)?} will apply the "?" quantifier to the entire pattern within the parentheses, matching "cats" or null string.

25.5.1 $1, $2, $3, etc Capturing parentheses

Clustering parentheses will also Capture the part of the string that matched the pattern within parentheses. The captured values are accessible through some "magical" variables called $1, $2, $3, ... Each left parenthesis increments the number used to access the captured string. The left parenthesis are counted from left to right as they occur within the pattern, starting at 1.

```
my $test="Firstname: John Lastname: Smith";
##################################################
#                    $1              $2
$test=~m{Firstname: (\w+) Lastname: (\w+)};
my $first = $1;
my $last = $2;
print "Hello, $first $last\n";
> Hello, John Smith
```

Because capturing takes a little extra time to store the captured result into the $1, $2, variables, sometimes you just want to cluster without the overhead of capturing. In the below example, we want to cluster "day|bye" so that the alternation symbol "|" will go with "day" or "bye". Without the clustering parenthesis, the pattern would match "goodday" or "bye", rather than "goodday" or "goodbye". The pattern contains capturing parens around the entire pattern, so we do not need to capture the "day|bye" part of the pattern, therefore we use cluster-only parentheses.

```
if($str =~ m{(good(?:day|bye))})
    {warn "group matched, captured '$1'";}
```

Cluster-only parenthesis don't capture the enclosed pattern, and they don't count when determining which magic variable, $1, $2, $3 ..., will contain the values from the capturing parentheses.

```perl
my $test = 'goodday John';
###############################################
#                   $1              $2
if($test =~ m{(good(?:day|bye)) (\w+)})
    { print "You said $1 to $2\n"; }

> You said goodday to John
```

25.5.2 Capturing parentheses not capturing

If a regular expression containing capturing parentheses does not match the string, the magic variables $1, $2, $3, etc will retain whatever PREVIOUS value they had from any PREVIOUS regular expression. This means that you MUST check to make sure the regular expression matches BEFORE you use the $1, $2, $3, etc variables.

In the example below, the second regular expression does not match, therefore $1 retains its old value of 'be'. Instead of printing out something like "Name is Horatio" or "Name is" and failing on an undefined value, perl instead keeps the old value for $1 and prints "Name is 'be'", instead.

```perl
my $string1 = 'To be, or not to be';
$string1 =~ m{not to (\w+)}; # matches, $1='be'
warn "The question is to $1";
my $string2 = 'that is the question';
$string2 =~ m{I knew him once, (\w+)}; # no match
warn "Name is '$1'";
# no match, so $1 retains its old value 'be'
> The question is to be at ./script.pl line 7.
> Name is 'be' at ./script.pl line 11.
```

25.6 *Character Classes*

The "." metacharacter will match any single character. This is equivalent to a character class that includes every possible character. You can easily define smaller character classes of your own using the square brackets []. Whatever characters are listed within the square brackets are part of that character class. Perl will then match any one character within that class.

```
[aeiouAEIOU] any vowel
[0123456789] any digit
```

25.6.1 Metacharacters Within Character Classes

Within the square brackets used to define a character class, all previously defined metacharacters cease to act as metacharacters and are interpreted as simple literal characters. Characters classes have their own special metacharacters.

\   (backslash) demeta the next character

-       (hyphen) Indicates a consecutive character range, inclusively.
        [a-f] indicates the letters a,b,c,d,e,f.
        Character ranges are based off of ASCII numeric values.

^   If it is the first character of the class, then this indicates the class
        is any character EXCEPT the ones in the square brackets.
        Warning: [^aeiou] means anything but a lower case vowel. This
        is not the same as "any consonant". The class [^aeiou] will
        match punctuation, numbers, and unicode characters.

25.7 Shortcut Character Classes

Perl has shortcut character classes for some more common classes.

Shortcut	class	description
\d	[0-9]	any digit
\D	[^0-9]	any NON-digit
\s	[\t\n\r\f]	any whitespace
\S	[^ \t\n\r\f]	any NON-whitespace
\w	[a-zA-Z0-9_]	any word character (valid perl identifier)
\W	[^a-zA-Z0-9_]	any NON-word character

25.8 Greedy (Maximal) Quantifiers

Quantifiers are used within regular expressions to indicate how many times the previous item occurs within the pattern. By default, quantifiers are "greedy" or "maximal", meaning that they will match as many characters as possible and still be true.

*	match zero or more times (match as much as possible)
+	match one or more times (match as much as possible)
?	match zero or one times (match as much as possible)
{count}	match exactly "count" times
{min, }	match at least "min" times (match as much as possible)
{min,max}	match at least "min" and at most "max" times (match as much as possible)

25.9 Thrifty (Minimal) Quantifiers

Placing a "?" after a quantifier disables greediness, making them "non-greedy", "thrifty", or "minimal" quantifiers. Minimal quantifiers match as few characters as possible and still be true.

*?	match zero or more times (match as little as possible and still be true)
+?	match one or more times (match as little as possible and still be true)
{min,}?	match at least min times (match as little as possible and still be true)
{min, max}?	match at least "min" and at most "max" times (match as little as possible and still be true)

This example shows the difference between minimal and maximal quantifiers.

```
my $string = "12340000";
if($string =~ m{^(\d+)0+$})
    { print "greedy '$1'\n"; }
if($string =~ m{^(\d+?)0+$})
    { print "thrifty '$1'\n"; }

> greedy '1234000'
> thrifty '1234'
```

25.10 Position Assertions / Position Anchors

Inside a regular expression pattern, some symbols do not translate into a character or character class. Instead, they translate into a "position" within the string. If a position anchor occurs within a pattern, the pattern before and after that anchor must occur within a certain position within the string.

^	Matches the beginning of the string. If the /m (multiline) modifier is present, matches "\n" also.
$	Matches the end of the string. If the /m (multiline) modifier is present, matches "\n" also.
\A	Match the beginning of string only. Not affected by /m modifier.
\z	Match the end of string only. Not affected by /m modifier.
\Z	Matches the end of the string only, but will chomp() a "\n" if that was the last character in string.
\b	word "b"oundary A word boundary occurs in four places. 1) at a transition from a \w character to a \W character 2) at a transition from a \W character to a \w character 3) at the beginning of the string 4) at the end of the string
\B	NOT \b
\G	usually used with /g modifier (probably want /c modifier too). Indicates the position after the character of the last pattern match performed on the string. If this is the first regular expression begin performed on the string then \G will match the beginning of the string. Use the pos() function to get and set the current \G position within the string.

25.10.1 The \b Anchor

Use the \b anchor when you want to match a whole word pattern but not part of a word. This example matches "jump" but not "jumprope":

```
my $test1='He can jump very high.';
if($test1=~m{\bjump\b})
   { print "test1 matches\n"; }

my $test2='Pick up that jumprope.';
unless($test2=~m{\bjump\b})
   { print "test2 does not match\n"; }

> test1 matches
> test2 does not match
```

25.10.2 The \G Anchor

The \G anchor is a sophisticated anchor used to perform a progression of many regular expression pattern matches on the same string. The \G anchor represents the position within the string where the previous regular expression finished. The first time a regular expression is performed on a string, the \G anchor represents the beginning of the string.

The location of the \G anchor within a string can be determined by calling the pos() function on the string. The pos() function will return the character index in the string (index zero is to the left of the first character in the string) representing the location of the \G anchor. Assigning to pos($str) will change the position of the \G anchor for that string.

The \G anchor is usually used with the "cg" modifiers. The "cg" modifiers tell perl to NOT reset the \G anchor to zero if the regular expression fails to match. This will allow a series of regular expressions to operate on a string, using the \G anchor to indicate the location where the previous regular expression finished. Without the "cg" modifiers, the first regular expression that fails to match will reset the \G anchor back to zero.

The example below uses the \G anchor to extract bits of information from a single string. After every regular expression, the script prints the pos() value of the string. Notice how the pos() value keeps increasing.

```
my $str = "Firstname: John Lastname: Smith
Bookcollection: Programming Perl, Perl Cookbook,
Impatient Perl";

if($str=~m{\GFirstname: (\w+) }cg) {
   my $first = $1;
   print "pos is ".pos($str)."\n";
}

if($str=~m{\GLastname: (\w+) }cg) {
   my $last = $1;
   print "pos is ".pos($str)."\n";
}

$str=~m{\GBookcollection: }cg;

while($str=~m{\G\s*([^,]+),?}cg) {
   print "book is '$1'\n";
   print "pos is ".pos($str)."\n";
}

> pos is 16
> pos is 32
> book is 'Programming Perl'
> pos is 65
> book is 'Perl Cookbook'
> pos is 80
> book is 'Impatient Perl'
> pos is 95
```

Another way to code the above script is to use substitution regular expressions and substitute each matched part with empty strings. The problem is that a substitution creates a new string and copies the remaining characters to that string, resulting in a much slower script. In the above example, the speed difference would not be noticeable to the user, but if you have a script that is parsing through a lot of text, the difference can be quite significant.

25.11 Modifiers

Regular expressions can take optional modifiers that tell perl additional information about how to interpret the regular expression. Modifiers are placed after the regular expression, outside any curly braces.

```
$str =~ m{pattern}modifiers;
$str =~ s{oldpatt}{newpatt}modifiers;
$str =~ tr{oldset}{newset}modifiers;
```

25.11.1 Global Modifiers

The following modifiers can be used with m{}, s{}{}, or tr{}{}.

- I   case Insensitive, m{cat}i matches cat, Cat, CaT, CAt, CAT, etc
- x   ignore spaces and tabs and carriage returns in pattern. This allows the pattern to be spread out over multiple lines and for regular perl comments to be inserted within the pattern but be ignored by the regular expression engine.
- S   treat string as a Single line.
  "." will match "\n" within the string.
  ^ and $ position anchors will only match literal beginning and end of string.
- M   treat string as Multiple lines. (DEFAULT)
  "." will NOT match "\n"
  ^ and $ position anchors will match literal beginning and end of string and also "\n" characters within the string.
  ^ and $ indicate start/end of "line" instead of start/end of string.
  ^ matches after "\n"
  $ matches before "\n"
- o   compile the pattern Once. possible speed improvement.

25.11.2 The m And s Modifiers

The default behavior of perl regular expressions is "m", treating strings as a multiple lines. If neither a "m" or "s" modifier is used on a regular expression, perl will default to "m" behavior.
If the "m" modifier is used, then the "^" anchor will match the beginning of the string or "\n" characters, the "$" anchor will match the end of the string or any "\n" characters, and the "." character set will match any character EXCEPT "\n". If a string contains multiple lines separated by "\n", then the default behavior (the "m" behavior) is to treat the string as multiple lines, using "^" and "$" to indicate start and end of lines.

If the "s" modifier is used, then the "^" anchor will only match the literal beginning of the string, the "$" anchor will only match the literal end of string, and the "." class will match any character including "\n". With the "s" modifier, even if the string is multiple lines with embedded "\n" characters, the "s" modifier forces perl to treat it as a single line.

This example shows the exact same pattern bound to the exact same string. The only difference is the modifier used on the regular expression. Notice in the "s" version, the captured string includes the newline "\n" characters which shows up in the printed output. The single line version prints out the captured pattern across three different lines.

```
my $string = "Library: Programming Perl \n"
            ."Perl Cookbook\n"
            ."Impatient Perl";
if($string =~ m{Library: (.*)})
   { print "default is '$1'\n"; }
if($string =~ m{Library: (.*)}m)
   { print "multiline is '$1'\n"; }
if($string =~ m{Library: (.*)}s)
   { print "singleline is '$1'\n"; }

> default is 'Programming Perl '
> multiline is 'Programming Perl '
> singleline is 'Programming Perl
> Perl Cookbook
> Impatient Perl
```

25.11.3 The x Modifier

The x modifier allows a complex regular expression pattern to be spread out over multiple lines, with comments, for easier reading. Most whitespace within a pattern with the x modifier is ignored. The following pattern is looking for a number that follows scientific notation. The pattern is spread out over multiple lines with comments to support maintainability.

```
my $string = '- 134.23423 e -12';
if( $string =~ m
{
    ^ \s* ([-+]?) # positive or negative or optional
    \s* ( \d+ ) # integer portion
        ( \. \d+ )? # fractional is optional
    ( \s* e \s* [+-]? \d+)? # exponent is optional
}x ) {
    my $sign       = $1 || '';
    my $integer    = $2 || '';
    my $fraction   = $3 || '';
    my $exponent   = $4 || '';

    print "sign is '$sign'\n";
    print "integer is '$integer'\n";
    print "fraction is '$fraction'\n";
    print "exponent is '$exponent'\n";
}

> sign is '-'
> integer is '134'
> fraction is '.23423'
> exponent is ' e -12'
```

A couple of notes for the above example: The x modifier strips out all spaces, tabs, and carriage returns in the pattern. If the pattern expects whitespace in the string, it must be explicitly stated using \s or \t or \n or some similar character class. Also, it's always a good idea to anchor your regular expression somewhere in your string, with "^" or "$" or "\G". The double-pipe expressions guarantee that the variables are assigned to whatever the pattern matched or empty string if no match occurred. Without them, an unmatched pattern match will yield an "undef" in the $1 (or $2 or $3) variable associated with the match.

25.12 Modifiers For m{} Operator

The following modifiers apply to the m{pattern} operator only:

    g   Globally find all matchs. Without this modifier, m{} will find the first occurrence of the pattern.
    cg   Continue search after Global search fails. This maintains the \G marker at its last matched position. Without this modifier, the \G marker is reset to zero if the pattern does not match.

25.13 Modifiers for s{}{} Operator

The following modifiers apply to the s{oldpatt}{newpatt} operator only.

    g   Globally replace all occurrences of oldpatt with newpatt
    e   interpret newpatt as a perl-based string Expression. the result of the expression becomes the replacement string.

25.14 Modifiers for tr{}{} Operator

The following modifiers apply to the tr{oldset}{newset} operator only.

    c   Complement the searchlist
    d   Delete found but unreplaced characters
    s   Squash duplicate replaced characters

25.15 The qr{} function

The qr{} function takes a string and interprets it as a regular expression, returning a value that can be stored in a scalar for pattern matching at a later time.
my $number = qr{[+-]?\s*\d+(?:\.\d+)?\s*(?:e\s*[+-]?\s*\d+)?};

25.16 Common Patterns

Some simple and common regular expression patterns are shown here:
```
        $str =~ s{\s}{}g; # remove all whitespace
        $str =~ s{#.*}{}; # remove perl comments
        next if($str =~ m{^\s*$});# next if only whitespace
```
For common but more complicated regular expressions, check out the Regexp::Common module on CPAN.

25.17 Regexp::Common

The Regexp::Common module contains many common, but fairly complicated, regular expression patterns (balanced parentheses and brackets, delimited text with escapes, integers and floating point numbers of different bases, email addresses, and others). If you are doing some complicated pattern matching, it might be worth a moment to check out Regexp::Common and see if someone already did the work to match the pattern you need.

```
> cpanm -i Regexp::Common
```

Once Regexp::Common is installed, perl scripts that use it will have a "magic" hash called %RE imported into their namespace. The keys to this hash are human understandable names, the data in the hash are the patterns to use within regular expressions.

Here is how to find out what the floating point number pattern looks like in Regexp::Common:

```
use Regexp::Common;
my $patt = $RE{num}{real};
print "$patt\n";

> (?:(?i)(?:[+-]?)(?:(?=[0123456789]|[.])(?:
[0123456789]*)(?:(?:[.])(?:[0123456789]{0,}))?)(?:
(?:[E])(?:(?:[+-]?)(?:[0123456789]+))|))
```

As complicated as this is, it is a lot easier to reuse someone else's code than to try and reinvent your own, faulty, lopsided, wheel.

The hash lookup can be used directly within your regular expression:

```
use Regexp::Common;
my $str = "this is -12.423E-42 the number";
$str =~ m{($RE{num}{real})};
print "match is '$1'\n";

> match is '-12.423E-42'
```

25.18 Regexp::Grammars

If Perl's regular expressions aren't sufficient to parse your text, you might want to look into Regexp::Grammar.

26 Perl, GUI, and Tk

So far, all the examples have had a command line interface. User input and output occurred through the same command line used to execute the perl script itself. Perl has a Graphical User Interface (GUI) toolkit module available on CPAN called Tk.

```
> cpanm -i Tk
```

The Tk module is a GUI toolkit that contains a plethora of buttons and labels and entry items and other widgets needed to create a graphical user interface to your scripts. Once installed, the Tk module has a widget demonstration program that can be run from the command line to see what widgets are available and what they look like. At the command line, type "widget" to run the demonstration program.

```
> widget
```

Here is a simple "hello world" style program using Tk:

```perl
use Tk;
my $top=new MainWindow;

$top->Button (
   -text=>"Hello",
   -command=>sub{print "Hi\n";}
)->grid(-row=>1,-column=>1);

MainLoop;
```

When the above example is executed, a small GUI will popup on the screen (the MainWindow item) with a button (the $top->Button call) labeled "Hello" (the -text option). When the mouse left-clicks on the button, the word "Hi" is printed to the command line (the -command option). The ->grid method invokes the geometry manager on the widget and places it somewhere in the GUI (without geometry management, the widget will not show up in the GUI). The MainLoop is a subroutine call that invokes the event loop, drawing the GUI, responding to button clicks, etc.

Several large books have been written about the Tk GUI toolkit for perl. And it would be impossible to give any decent introduction to this module in a page or two. If you plan on creating GUI's in your scripts, I recommend the "Mastering Perl/Tk" book.

27 GNU Free Documentation License

GNU Free Documentation License
Version 1.3, 3 November 2008

Copyright (C) 2000, 2001, 2002, 2007, 2008 Free Software Foundation, Inc.
 <http://fsf.org/>
Everyone is permitted to copy and distribute verbatim copies
of this license document, but changing it is not allowed.

0. PREAMBLE

The purpose of this License is to make a manual, textbook, or other
functional and useful document "free" in the sense of freedom: to
assure everyone the effective freedom to copy and redistribute it,
with or without modifying it, either commercially or noncommercially.
Secondarily, this License preserves for the author and publisher a way
to get credit for their work, while not being considered responsible
for modifications made by others.

This License is a kind of "copyleft", which means that derivative
works of the document must themselves be free in the same sense. It
complements the GNU General Public License, which is a copyleft
license designed for free software.

We have designed this License in order to use it for manuals for free
software, because free software needs free documentation: a free
program should come with manuals providing the same freedoms that the
software does. But this License is not limited to software manuals;
it can be used for any textual work, regardless of subject matter or
whether it is published as a printed book. We recommend this License
principally for works whose purpose is instruction or reference.

1. APPLICABILITY AND DEFINITIONS

This License applies to any manual or other work, in any medium, that
contains a notice placed by the copyright holder saying it can be
distributed under the terms of this License. Such a notice grants a
world-wide, royalty-free license, unlimited in duration, to use that
work under the conditions stated herein. The "Document", below,
refers to any such manual or work. Any member of the public is a
licensee, and is addressed as "you". You accept the license if you
copy, modify or distribute the work in a way requiring permission
under copyright law.

A "Modified Version" of the Document means any work containing the

Document or a portion of it, either copied verbatim, or with modifications and/or translated into another language.

A "Secondary Section" is a named appendix or a front-matter section of the Document that deals exclusively with the relationship of the publishers or authors of the Document to the Document's overall subject (or to related matters) and contains nothing that could fall directly within that overall subject. (Thus, if the Document is in part a textbook of mathematics, a Secondary Section may not explain any mathematics.) The relationship could be a matter of historical connection with the subject or with related matters, or of legal, commercial, philosophical, ethical or political position regarding them.

The "Invariant Sections" are certain Secondary Sections whose titles are designated, as being those of Invariant Sections, in the notice that says that the Document is released under this License. If a section does not fit the above definition of Secondary then it is not allowed to be designated as Invariant. The Document may contain zero Invariant Sections. If the Document does not identify any Invariant Sections then there are none.

The "Cover Texts" are certain short passages of text that are listed, as Front-Cover Texts or Back-Cover Texts, in the notice that says that the Document is released under this License. A Front-Cover Text may be at most 5 words, and a Back-Cover Text may be at most 25 words.

A "Transparent" copy of the Document means a machine-readable copy, represented in a format whose specification is available to the general public, that is suitable for revising the document straightforwardly with generic text editors or (for images composed of pixels) generic paint programs or (for drawings) some widely available drawing editor, and that is suitable for input to text formatters or for automatic translation to a variety of formats suitable for input to text formatters. A copy made in an otherwise Transparent file format whose markup, or absence of markup, has been arranged to thwart or discourage subsequent modification by readers is not Transparent. An image format is not Transparent if used for any substantial amount of text. A copy that is not "Transparent" is called "Opaque".

Examples of suitable formats for Transparent copies include plain ASCII without markup, Texinfo input format, LaTeX input format, SGML or XML using a publicly available DTD, and standard-conforming simple HTML, PostScript or PDF designed for human modification. Examples of transparent image formats include PNG, XCF and JPG. Opaque formats include proprietary formats that can be read and edited only by proprietary word processors, SGML or XML for which the DTD and/or processing tools are not generally available, and the machine-generated HTML, PostScript or PDF produced by some word processors for output purposes only.

The "Title Page" means, for a printed book, the title page itself, plus such following pages as are needed to hold, legibly, the material this License requires to appear in the title page. For works in formats which do not have any title page as such, "Title Page" means the text near the most prominent appearance of the work's title, preceding the beginning of the body of the text.

The "publisher" means any person or entity that distributes copies of the Document to the public.

A section "Entitled XYZ" means a named subunit of the Document whose title either is precisely XYZ or contains XYZ in parentheses following text that translates XYZ in another language. (Here XYZ stands for a specific section name mentioned below, such as "Acknowledgements", "Dedications", "Endorsements", or "History".) To "Preserve the Title" of such a section when you modify the Document means that it remains a section "Entitled XYZ" according to this definition.

The Document may include Warranty Disclaimers next to the notice which states that this License applies to the Document. These Warranty Disclaimers are considered to be included by reference in this License, but only as regards disclaiming warranties: any other implication that these Warranty Disclaimers may have is void and has no effect on the meaning of this License.

2. VERBATIM COPYING

You may copy and distribute the Document in any medium, either commercially or noncommercially, provided that this License, the copyright notices, and the license notice saying this License applies to the Document are reproduced in all copies, and that you add no other conditions whatsoever to those of this License. You may not use technical measures to obstruct or control the reading or further copying of the copies you make or distribute. However, you may accept compensation in exchange for copies. If you distribute a large enough number of copies you must also follow the conditions in section 3.

You may also lend copies, under the same conditions stated above, and you may publicly display copies.

3. COPYING IN QUANTITY

If you publish printed copies (or copies in media that commonly have printed covers) of the Document, numbering more than 100, and the

Document's license notice requires Cover Texts, you must enclose the
copies in covers that carry, clearly and legibly, all these Cover
Texts: Front-Cover Texts on the front cover, and Back-Cover Texts on
the back cover. Both covers must also clearly and legibly identify
you as the publisher of these copies. The front cover must present
the full title with all words of the title equally prominent and
visible. You may add other material on the covers in addition.
Copying with changes limited to the covers, as long as they preserve
the title of the Document and satisfy these conditions, can be treated
as verbatim copying in other respects.

If the required texts for either cover are too voluminous to fit
legibly, you should put the first ones listed (as many as fit
reasonably) on the actual cover, and continue the rest onto adjacent
pages.

If you publish or distribute Opaque copies of the Document numbering
more than 100, you must either include a machine-readable Transparent
copy along with each Opaque copy, or state in or with each Opaque copy
a computer-network location from which the general network-using
public has access to download using public-standard network protocols
a complete Transparent copy of the Document, free of added material.
If you use the latter option, you must take reasonably prudent steps,
when you begin distribution of Opaque copies in quantity, to ensure
that this Transparent copy will remain thus accessible at the stated
location until at least one year after the last time you distribute an
Opaque copy (directly or through your agents or retailers) of that
edition to the public.

It is requested, but not required, that you contact the authors of the
Document well before redistributing any large number of copies, to
give them a chance to provide you with an updated version of the
Document.

4. MODIFICATIONS

You may copy and distribute a Modified Version of the Document under
the conditions of sections 2 and 3 above, provided that you release
the Modified Version under precisely this License, with the Modified
Version filling the role of the Document, thus licensing distribution
and modification of the Modified Version to whoever possesses a copy
of it. In addition, you must do these things in the Modified Version:

A. Use in the Title Page (and on the covers, if any) a title distinct
   from that of the Document, and from those of previous versions
   (which should, if there were any, be listed in the History section
   of the Document). You may use the same title as a previous version

if the original publisher of that version gives permission.
B. List on the Title Page, as authors, one or more persons or entities responsible for authorship of the modifications in the Modified Version, together with at least five of the principal authors of the Document (all of its principal authors, if it has fewer than five), unless they release you from this requirement.
C. State on the Title page the name of the publisher of the Modified Version, as the publisher.
D. Preserve all the copyright notices of the Document.
E. Add an appropriate copyright notice for your modifications adjacent to the other copyright notices.
F. Include, immediately after the copyright notices, a license notice giving the public permission to use the Modified Version under the terms of this License, in the form shown in the Addendum below.
G. Preserve in that license notice the full lists of Invariant Sections and required Cover Texts given in the Document's license notice.
H. Include an unaltered copy of this License.
I. Preserve the section Entitled "History", Preserve its Title, and add to it an item stating at least the title, year, new authors, and publisher of the Modified Version as given on the Title Page. If there is no section Entitled "History" in the Document, create one stating the title, year, authors, and publisher of the Document as given on its Title Page, then add an item describing the Modified Version as stated in the previous sentence.
J. Preserve the network location, if any, given in the Document for public access to a Transparent copy of the Document, and likewise the network locations given in the Document for previous versions it was based on. These may be placed in the "History" section. You may omit a network location for a work that was published at least four years before the Document itself, or if the original publisher of the version it refers to gives permission.
K. For any section Entitled "Acknowledgements" or "Dedications", Preserve the Title of the section, and preserve in the section all the substance and tone of each of the contributor acknowledgements and/or dedications given therein.
L. Preserve all the Invariant Sections of the Document, unaltered in their text and in their titles. Section numbers or the equivalent are not considered part of the section titles.
M. Delete any section Entitled "Endorsements". Such a section may not be included in the Modified Version.
N. Do not retitle any existing section to be Entitled "Endorsements" or to conflict in title with any Invariant Section.
O. Preserve any Warranty Disclaimers.

If the Modified Version includes new front-matter sections or appendices that qualify as Secondary Sections and contain no material copied from the Document, you may at your option designate some or all of these sections as invariant. To do this, add their titles to the

list of Invariant Sections in the Modified Version's license notice.
These titles must be distinct from any other section titles.

You may add a section Entitled "Endorsements", provided it contains
nothing but endorsements of your Modified Version by various
parties--for example, statements of peer review or that the text has
been approved by an organization as the authoritative definition of a
standard.

You may add a passage of up to five words as a Front-Cover Text, and a
passage of up to 25 words as a Back-Cover Text, to the end of the list
of Cover Texts in the Modified Version. Only one passage of
Front-Cover Text and one of Back-Cover Text may be added by (or
through arrangements made by) any one entity. If the Document already
includes a cover text for the same cover, previously added by you or
by arrangement made by the same entity you are acting on behalf of,
you may not add another; but you may replace the old one, on explicit
permission from the previous publisher that added the old one.

The author(s) and publisher(s) of the Document do not by this License
give permission to use their names for publicity for or to assert or
imply endorsement of any Modified Version.

5. COMBINING DOCUMENTS

You may combine the Document with other documents released under this
License, under the terms defined in section 4 above for modified
versions, provided that you include in the combination all of the
Invariant Sections of all of the original documents, unmodified, and
list them all as Invariant Sections of your combined work in its
license notice, and that you preserve all their Warranty Disclaimers.

The combined work need only contain one copy of this License, and
multiple identical Invariant Sections may be replaced with a single
copy. If there are multiple Invariant Sections with the same name but
different contents, make the title of each such section unique by
adding at the end of it, in parentheses, the name of the original
author or publisher of that section if known, or else a unique number.
Make the same adjustment to the section titles in the list of
Invariant Sections in the license notice of the combined work.

In the combination, you must combine any sections Entitled "History"
in the various original documents, forming one section Entitled
"History"; likewise combine any sections Entitled "Acknowledgements",
and any sections Entitled "Dedications". You must delete all sections
Entitled "Endorsements".

6. COLLECTIONS OF DOCUMENTS

You may make a collection consisting of the Document and other documents released under this License, and replace the individual copies of this License in the various documents with a single copy that is included in the collection, provided that you follow the rules of this License for verbatim copying of each of the documents in all other respects.

You may extract a single document from such a collection, and distribute it individually under this License, provided you insert a copy of this License into the extracted document, and follow this License in all other respects regarding verbatim copying of that document.

7. AGGREGATION WITH INDEPENDENT WORKS

A compilation of the Document or its derivatives with other separate and independent documents or works, in or on a volume of a storage or distribution medium, is called an "aggregate" if the copyright resulting from the compilation is not used to limit the legal rights of the compilation's users beyond what the individual works permit. When the Document is included in an aggregate, this License does not apply to the other works in the aggregate which are not themselves derivative works of the Document.

If the Cover Text requirement of section 3 is applicable to these copies of the Document, then if the Document is less than one half of the entire aggregate, the Document's Cover Texts may be placed on covers that bracket the Document within the aggregate, or the electronic equivalent of covers if the Document is in electronic form. Otherwise they must appear on printed covers that bracket the whole aggregate.

8. TRANSLATION

Translation is considered a kind of modification, so you may distribute translations of the Document under the terms of section 4. Replacing Invariant Sections with translations requires special permission from their copyright holders, but you may include translations of some or all Invariant Sections in addition to the original versions of these Invariant Sections. You may include a translation of this License, and all the license notices in the Document, and any Warranty Disclaimers, provided that you also include the original English version of this License and the original versions of those notices and disclaimers. In case of a disagreement between

the translation and the original version of this License or a notice
or disclaimer, the original version will prevail.

If a section in the Document is Entitled "Acknowledgements",
"Dedications", or "History", the requirement (section 4) to Preserve
its Title (section 1) will typically require changing the actual
title.

9. TERMINATION

You may not copy, modify, sublicense, or distribute the Document
except as expressly provided under this License. Any attempt
otherwise to copy, modify, sublicense, or distribute it is void, and
will automatically terminate your rights under this License.

However, if you cease all violation of this License, then your license
from a particular copyright holder is reinstated (a) provisionally,
unless and until the copyright holder explicitly and finally
terminates your license, and (b) permanently, if the copyright holder
fails to notify you of the violation by some reasonable means prior to
60 days after the cessation.

Moreover, your license from a particular copyright holder is
reinstated permanently if the copyright holder notifies you of the
violation by some reasonable means, this is the first time you have
received notice of violation of this License (for any work) from that
copyright holder, and you cure the violation prior to 30 days after
your receipt of the notice.

Termination of your rights under this section does not terminate the
licenses of parties who have received copies or rights from you under
this License. If your rights have been terminated and not permanently
reinstated, receipt of a copy of some or all of the same material does
not give you any rights to use it.

10. FUTURE REVISIONS OF THIS LICENSE

The Free Software Foundation may publish new, revised versions of the
GNU Free Documentation License from time to time. Such new versions
will be similar in spirit to the present version, but may differ in
detail to address new problems or concerns. See
http://www.gnu.org/copyleft/.

Each version of the License is given a distinguishing version number.
If the Document specifies that a particular numbered version of this
License "or any later version" applies to it, you have the option of

following the terms and conditions either of that specified version or
of any later version that has been published (not as a draft) by the
Free Software Foundation. If the Document does not specify a version
number of this License, you may choose any version ever published (not
as a draft) by the Free Software Foundation. If the Document
specifies that a proxy can decide which future versions of this
License can be used, that proxy's public statement of acceptance of a
version permanently authorizes you to choose that version for the
Document.

11. RELICENSING

"Massive Multiauthor Collaboration Site" (or "MMC Site") means any
World Wide Web server that publishes copyrightable works and also
provides prominent facilities for anybody to edit those works. A
public wiki that anybody can edit is an example of such a server. A
"Massive Multiauthor Collaboration" (or "MMC") contained in the site
means any set of copyrightable works thus published on the MMC site.

"CC-BY-SA" means the Creative Commons Attribution-Share Alike 3.0
license published by Creative Commons Corporation, a not-for-profit
corporation with a principal place of business in San Francisco,
California, as well as future copyleft versions of that license
published by that same organization.

"Incorporate" means to publish or republish a Document, in whole or in
part, as part of another Document.

An MMC is "eligible for relicensing" if it is licensed under this
License, and if all works that were first published under this License
somewhere other than this MMC, and subsequently incorporated in whole or
in part into the MMC, (1) had no cover texts or invariant sections, and
(2) were thus incorporated prior to November 1, 2008.

The operator of an MMC Site may republish an MMC contained in the site
under CC-BY-SA on the same site at any time before August 1, 2009,
provided the MMC is eligible for relicensing.

ADDENDUM: How to use this License for your documents

To use this License in a document you have written, include a copy of
the License in the document and put the following copyright and
license notices just after the title page:

    Copyright (c) YEAR YOUR NAME.
    Permission is granted to copy, distribute and/or modify this document
    under the terms of the GNU Free Documentation License, Version 1.3

or any later version published by the Free Software Foundation;
with no Invariant Sections, no Front-Cover Texts, and no Back-Cover Texts.
A copy of the license is included in the section entitled "GNU
Free Documentation License".

If you have Invariant Sections, Front-Cover Texts and Back-Cover Texts,
replace the "with...Texts." line with this:

with the Invariant Sections being LIST THEIR TITLES, with the
Front-Cover Texts being LIST, and with the Back-Cover Texts being LIST.

If you have Invariant Sections without Cover Texts, or some other
combination of the three, merge those two alternatives to suit the
situation.

If your document contains nontrivial examples of program code, we
recommend releasing these examples in parallel under your choice of
free software license, such as the GNU General Public License,
to permit their use in free software.

Alphabetical Index

abs	18
anonymous	56
anonymous subroutine	77
anonymous subroutines	75
argument passing	77
array	35
@	35
$	35
Autovivification	58
backtick	122
base conversion	24
BEGIN	84
bless	91p.
bless / constructors	107
bless REFERENCE, STRING	91
blessed invocant	98
boolean	26
caller	82
can	97
Capturing and Clustering Parenthesis	129
Character Classes	130
CHECK	84
chomp	14
class	102
clone	60
close	118
closures	72
code reference	79
code reuse	86
command line	
Getopt	
:Declare	115
@ARGV	112
Command Line Arguments	112
comparison operator	28
compiling	84
complex data structures	57
concatenation	15
conditional operator	31
continue	64
control flow	64
cos	19
CPAN	110
CPAN, The Web Site	110
Creating Modules	111
Data Persistence	60

dclone	60
deep clone	60
defined	25
delete	45
dereference	54
dereferencing code references	79
double quote	14
e	20
each	47
else	64
elsif	64
END	84
execution timeline	90
exists	44
exp	20
exponentiation	20
false	26
File	
Find	121
file glob	120
File Input and Output	118
File IO	
close	118
read	119
write	120
File Test	
-e	120
-l	120
-p	120
-w	120
File Tests	120
for	64
foreach	39, 64
garbage collection	70p.
Getopt	
Declare	115
glob	120
Global Modifiers	136
Global Modifiers (regular expressions)	136
Greedy (Maximal) Quantifiers	132
GUI and Perl	
Tk	141
hash	43
$	43
here document	17
hex	23
hexadecimal	18
imaginary numbers	20

import	87, 89
Inheritance	95, 108
INIT	84
int	19
interpreting	84
INVOCANT -> METHOD	93
INVOCANT->can(METHODNAME)	97
INVOCANT->isa(BASEPACKAGE)	97
isa	97
keys	46
label	65
last	65
length	15
lexical scope	68
lexical variable	69
list	51
literal	
binary	18
hexadecimal	18
octal	18
string	14
local	75
log	20
logical operators	29
m/patt/	124
Math	
Complex	20
Trig	19
Metacharacters Within Character Classes	131
method calls	93
Methods	108
Modules	106
multidimensional array	59
multiline string	17
named referent	54
named subroutine	75
named subroutines	75
namespace	66
natural logarithms	20
next	65
nstore	60
numbers	18
numeric	
literal	18
rounding	19
numify	23
Object Destruction	105
object oriented perl	91

Object Oriented Perl	99
Object Oriented Review	106
oct	23
octal	18
open	118
23 Operating System Commands	122
backtick	122
system	122
Tk	
:ExecuteCommand	123
`	122
our	67
Overriding Methods	109
package	66
package main	66
package qualified variable	66
perl modules	86
PERL5LIB	88
pop	37
Position Assertions / Position Anchors	133
push	37
quote	
doube	14
single	14
qw	14, 16
rand	21
random numbers	21
read	119
redo	65
ref	62, 92
reference	53
referent	53, 92
Regexp	
Common	140
24 Regular Expressions	124
alternation	127
capturing	127
Capturing and Clustering Parenthesis	129
Character Classes	130
clustering	127
Defining a Pattern	126
Global Modifiers	136
Greedy (Maximal) Quantifiers	132
grouping	127
m/patt/	124
Metacharacters	127
Position Assertions / Position Anchors	133
quantifier	127

    Shortcut Character Classes..131
    Thrifty (Minimal) Quantifiers..132
    Variable Interpolation..125
    Wildcard Example...126
    !~...124
    =~..124
    $1, $2, $3...129
require..87, 89
retrieve..60
return..80
reuse..86
rounding...19
scalar..36
    Autovivify..13
    numbers...18
    string..14
    $..13
shift..38
Shortcut Character Classes..131
sin..19
single quote...14
sort...40
spaceship operator..28
splice...42
sprintf..22
sqrt..20
srand..21
Storable.pm...60
string...
    double quote..14
    single quote...14
stringify...22
subroutine...
    argument passing..77
subroutine closures..72
subroutine return value..80
subroutines..75
    anonymous..75
    closures...72
    named..75
system..122
ternary operator...31
Thrifty (Minimal) Quantifiers...132
Tk...
    ExecuteCommand...123
trinary operator..31
true...26
undefined...25

unshift	38
use	87
use base MODULENAME	96
use lib	88
use Module	106
use MODULENAME	87
values	46
wantarray	83
while	64
write	120
'	14, 134
-d	120
-e	120
-f	120
-r	120
-S	120
-T	120
-x	120
-z	120
!~	124
?	31
'	14
[]	130
@	35
@_	78
@ARGV	113
@INC	88
@ISA	96
**	20
<<	17
<$fh>	119
=~	124
$	13
scalar	13
$1, $2, $3	129

The End.